LOVING ENOUGH TO CARE

LOVING ENOUGH TO CARE

EARL D. WILSON

MULTNOMAH PRESS
PORTLAND, OREGON 97266

Cover Design by Hilber Nelson

LOVING ENOUGH TO CARE
© 1984 by Multnomah Press
Printed in the United States of America

First printing 1984

Library of Congress Cataloging in Publication Data

Wilson, Earl D., 1939-
    Loving enough to care, it could change your life!

    Includes bibliographical references.
    1. Caring—Moral and ethical aspects.   I. Title.
BJ1475.W54   1983   248.4.   83-27053
ISBN 0-88070-040-8 (pbk.)

Dedication

—

To Sandy, my wife,
thanks for caring for me so freely
and for being patient enough
to help me to learn to care for you
and others. You have loved me
through laughter and tears—
no person could ask for more.

Contents

Foreword

I used to think I was a caring person.

Recently, I've realized that many times I care for my friends and loved ones in ways that are convenient for me and make me feel good about myself. *Loving Enough to Care* points the reader in a different direction, however.

I originally asked Dr. Wilson to write this book. As his secretary and friend, I had the opportunity to watch him and his wife Sandy develop into very caring people. And I asked them to teach me how to care.

Now in this book, Dr. Wilson offers hope that caring is a skill to be learned. It requires patience and perseverance. True caring asks for a commitment to love and serve at times and in ways that aren't always easy or convenient. It is listening and observing a person long enough to determine his or her needs and how he or she can best *hear* and *receive* caring from me. It makes a statement that says, "You have value. I care enough to get to know who *you* are and how I can best meet the need you have." Sometimes the hardest thing to do is to find creative ways to walk beside those we love as they struggle and grow.

Out of his personal experiences, Dr. Wilson shares ideas, strategies, and encouragement. Then he gives us a view of the God who enables us to do all things, the God who cares.

Kay Quick

1

In Search of the Lost Treasure

Where have we missed God's plan?

W E FLEW TO the remote Mexican village in the middle of the afternoon. There were ten of us—five children and five adults. The natives just shook their heads as they watched us trudge up the long trail to the home of missionaries Jim and Nadine Rupp. Their three small rooms would never be the same.

When we retired for the night, we were wall-to-wall people. Gene Congdon, our pilot and friend, slept under the table with his son Todd close by his side. Our son Mark, age ten, curled up on the concrete floor near us with his sister and brother next to him. He gripped his hand tightly as he slept. In it was his newest treasure, a silver ring he had purchased with his own money at Taxco, the silver capital of Mexico. He was proud of the ring. It was like a new friend.

When we awoke the next morning, Nadine served our whole group a nice breakfast. The children ran to play while we enjoyed a second cup of rich Mexican coffee. Suddenly our conversation was interrupted by a cry. We went out and found Mark sobbing; he frantically scoured the ground with his eyes.

"My ring, my ring," he cried, "It's gone. My new ring is lost."

We all joined the search, but after a half hour, I called it off. It was hard to tell Mark we had to leave; it meant his treasure

11

had to be abandoned, lost forever. He accepted the loss as graciously as a ten-year-old could, and we packed up to hike to the cowpath that doubled as an airstrip. Jim Rupp walked us to the plane, but Nadine stayed behind to take care of some urgent task in her busy schedule.

Gene had planned two flights to get us back to Metla. Mark, Mike, and I helped by coaxing, herding, and chasing a few donkeys off the primitive airstrip so that the takeoff and landing would be safe. As the plane circled overhead on its return from the first trip, we heard a shout in the distance. Jim recognized the voice. "It's Nadine," he said. "She is almost to the clearing." We moved to meet her and could hear her more clearly.

"Mark," she yelled, "I have your ring."

Excitement wouldn't allow him to hold back. He ran to meet Nadine and to touch and admire his lost ring, his treasure. The plane landed, and as Gene readied the aircraft for the second takeoff, we learned the whole story.

Nadine's important job was to find Mark's lost treasure. She had crawled on her hands and knees in the mud, carefully sorting the tall grass until she found the silver band. What a unique act of caring! Nadine found Mark's treasure, it is true; but the greater Treasure was what she displayed—the art of caring.

This book is about Nadine's treasure. Many of us seem to have lost it. We don't know how to care for people, even those we love the most.

What is caring? I define caring as being sensitive enough to others to meet some of their needs. Some have called caring "love in action." I care for you when, knowing who you are, I seek to help you to become all you can be. Caring is not just wishing people well or having interest or concern. Caring includes a commitment to helping people grow.

In preparing for a seminar, *Caring for Your Spouse*, which I do jointly with my wife, Sandy, I discovered an important definition of caring in, of all places, the dictionary. Webster says that caring is "a painstaking or watchful attention, a burdensome sense of responsibility." This definition points out how dedicated genuine caring is.

You don't have to be a social scientist or even a skilled people observer to know that caring for others is a rare commodity, even in the Christian family. As persons, we are complete in Christ. He is all we need in life. But God has determined that we fulfill each other by meeting needs within our relationships—by caring for one another. To care is to love in the most active sense. "All men will know that you are my disciples if you love one another" (John 13:35).

In the book of Genesis we learn that God invented the family as a response to the loneliness of man. "The LORD God said, 'It is not good for the man to be alone. I will make a helper suitable for him' " (Genesis 2:18). Yet in the late twentieth century, some of the loneliest people in the world are married. The treasure of caring has been lost.

Mike sat in my office soberly relating some of the history of his life with Linda. "It was so perfect at first," he said. "I had made a list of characteristics for the 'perfect' woman for me. She met all fourteen or fifteen things on the list. I may have restated a few of the points in her favor, but she was the perfect person for me. When we married it was dynamite. My emotions followed my decision and it was fantastic."

Mike and I labored together like archaeologists trying to find the fragments of a broken piece of pottery. In only a few years the perfect marriage had shattered to fragments. Mike reported that during the last year, the marriage was plagued by fights, name calling, and constant threats of divorce.

"What could I have done to make something so beautiful turn out so badly?" Mike wondered about his caring skills; he wondered about his emotions. His mind was plagued with the ruthless question, "Where did I go wrong?"

Linda, too, seemed to have lost her ability to care. Instead of always being the beautiful, vivacious, sympathetic person he married, she was at times short-tempered, caustic, and unforgiving. Caring is a skill that flows out of an attitude of love. Such skills may be dulled or lost completely if they are not exercised and cultivated.

Paul exhorts husbands to love their wives as Christ loved the church. He admonishes wives to follow the leadership of their husbands and to serve as helpmates. Children read about honoring their father and mother. Parents learn not to provoke their children to wrath. Friends find the urging to exercise friendship. These commands demand responsible and watchful caring for those you love.

Loving Your Neighbor as Yourself:
Three Steps to Caring

One of the significant keys to caring centers in the Matthew 19:19 command. Jesus instructed the rich young man to "love your neighbor as yourself."

What would it require to fulfill such a request? To love or care for someone, you need to know his needs. You can't even love yourself without a working understanding of who you are and what you need.

Bill told me how much he wanted to care for his wife and family, but he couldn't figure out why family members were so unhappy. When I talked to his wife and son, they both gave the same response. "He really doesn't take the time to know what we need. He thinks bringing home a healthy paycheck means he is caring for us. He is wrong!"

Bill lacked understanding of his family and their needs; he didn't lack the desire to express caring. He worked hard. He had to learn to listen to them and to speak with compassion. It hasn't been easy, but he has made great progress.

Caring shows itself in a second way—action. Caring without action is dead. Good intentions are not enough. If you love yourself, you actively care for your body, mind, and spirit. In expressing how husbands are to love their wives, Paul emphasizes, "After all, no one ever hated his own body, but he feeds and cares for it, just as Christ does the church" (Ephesians 5:29).

For years I had wanted to do a better job of showing Sandy just how much I appreciated her as a wife, mother, and God's special gift to me. I had lots of warm thoughts, but I didn't communicate them to her. The action step was missing.

Slowly but surely I have begun to write myself notes and rearrange my schedule to make sure caring comes first. Sandy feels cared for now with active steps like the card habit. Often I stand at a card rack in the drugstore next to my office, laughing out loud as I find the message that will communicate best with her.

Caring evaporates in vain promises. When Sandy was very ill, our friend Linda came to see her. That was active caring. But on her way out, Linda said, as people often do, "If there is anything I can do for you, don't hesitate to call." She left, and Sandy returned to the couch to rest.

About thirty minutes later, Linda reappeared at the door. This time she was wearing jeans. After she came in and glanced around a few corners, she began tucking up her sleeves. "Where's your mop? On the way home God showed me how silly I had been. I asked for you to call me if you needed anything, but I realized on the way home that you don't have the strength to do your housework."

Linda had transformed glib statements about a willingness to care into concrete action. Her love and caring was felt—and felt very deeply.

Perseverance is a third way to keep it going as a person who cares. You spend more than four hours per day in caring for yourself—eating, bathing, relaxing, praying. You repeat this personal caring over and over again as the days pass on. This type of ongoing commitment is a part of effective caring. A lack of steady, planned time with others is usually a sign that the treasure of caring has been lost.

I am not suggesting that you spend four hours each day caring for your friend or even for a family member. If you are honest, you will realize that the time you spend in caring for each member of your family could be measured in minutes, not hours. I was appalled to learn that most parents spend less than thirty seconds per day in conversation with one child alone. This is scary because time with parents is one form of caring children need most.

Over and over again I hear couples complain that they just don't talk. Single people complain that their friends never call and that there is no steady input into the relationship. Persistence is a hallmark of caring. Galatians 6 gives us a detailed prescription about how to care for a brother who is having problems with sin. Paul offers strong words of encouragement. "Let us not become weary in doing good, for at the proper time we will reap a harvest if we do not give up. Therefore, as we have opportunity, let us do good to all people, especially to those who belong to the family of believers" (Galatians 6:9, 10).

To care—to love your neighbor as yourself—you must develop the characteristics of understanding, action, and perseverance. The purpose of this book is to help you find this lost treasure and polish it until it shines prominently in your daily life.

How will we know the treasure when we find it? What does it look like? Carefully examining an effective caring relationship can begin our search. The book of Ruth presents a starting point and a picture of just what we're looking for.

Ruth and Naomi: A Case Study in Caring

> "Don't call me Naomi," she told them. "Call me Mara, because the Almighty has made my life very bitter. I went away full, but the LORD has brought me back empty. Why call me Naomi? The LORD has afflicted me; the Almighty has brought misfortune upon me" (Ruth 1:20-21).

The above statement frightens many Christians. It paints a vivid picture of a perplexing problem. How could a follower of God experience such a deep state of disappointment and depression that she would no longer permit people to call her by her name, Naomi (Pleasantness), and instead demanded to be called Mara (Bitter)? Reality tells us that our churches and homes are filled with bitter persons, despondent over their circumstances. How should we who desire to serve God and others react to the hurts we see in those around us? How can we care for them?

An investigation of the entire book of Ruth will turn up our answers. If we consider Naomi as a representative of all needy persons, and Ruth as God's person who cares for others, we will find the process—the exciting process—of caring acted out for us.

Does Ruth's interaction with Naomi include vital elements of care which God uses to help Naomi overcome her dark situation? What are the distinctive features which Ruth demonstrates as a caring person? First, notice Ruth's strong commitment to Naomi.

> At this they wept again. Then Orpah kissed her mother-in-law good-by, but Ruth clung to her.
> "Look," said Naomi, "your sister-in-law is going back to her people and her gods. Go back with her."
> But Ruth replied, "Don't urge me to leave you or to turn back from you. Where you go I will go, and where you stay I will stay. Your people will be my people and your God my God. Where you die I will die, and there I will be buried. May the LORD deal with me, be it ever so

severely, if anything but death separates you and me."
When Naomi realized that Ruth was determined to go
with her, she stopped urging her (Ruth 1:14-18).

Ruth cared enough to stay with Naomi even in the face of
uncertainty and discouragement. Staying close to your friend
or family member is very important. People need care even
when they cannot seem to care for themselves. Initially both
Ruth and Orpah had great love and concern for Naomi. In the
final analysis, however, Ruth cared enough to be involved
beyond the talking stage. Orpah returned home. Ruth was
not only aware of Naomi's need but was determined to be
used of God to meet that need, even if she didn't have any
quick solutions.

Second, Ruth initiated action. Needy persons are often im-
mobile persons. Even in the face of starvation, Naomi did not
seem to be able to take hold of herself in order to provide her
own basic needs. She responded impassively to Ruth's request to take some action.

> And Ruth the Moabitess said to Naomi, "Let me go to
> the fields and pick up the leftover grain behind anyone
> in whose eyes I find favor." Naomi said to her, "Go
> ahead, my daughter" (Ruth 2:2).

Don't get discouraged if your attempts to care for a depressed individual are not met with enthusiasm. The text
seems to indicate that after Ruth had initiated action and had
brought home the tangible fruits of her caring, Naomi's interest in life began to be rekindled. See Ruth 2:19, 20.

Third, notice that Ruth never labeled Naomi a "sicko." She
treated her with respect, sought her advice, and followed her
suggestions. This was undoubtedly a prime factor in restor-
ing Naomi's confidence. Feelings of unworthiness and loss of
personal respect are common problems of needy persons, the
severely depressed or the mildly discouraged. Expressing a
strong attitude of respect toward persons who are in need
will enable them to respect themselves and unravel their
"web of concerns." This happened to Naomi.

In chapter 3 of Ruth we see even stronger signs of Naomi's
recovery. She began to exercise herself and to take some responsibility for herself and for Ruth.

> One day Naomi her mother-in-law said to her, "My daughter, should I not try to find a home for you, where you will be well provided for?" (Ruth 3:1).

Think of it! You have patiently and persistently cared for someone else and, all of a sudden, this person begins to care for you in return. A person who was viewed as sick may emerge as a strong source of support for the one who took the time to care first.

Remember this fourth factor in caring for your friend or family member: Recognize and encourage competency. Ruth apparently recognized Naomi's emerging competence and her wisdom, and thus the Moabitess was willing to adopt her plan and to lend encouragement to her ideas. What a sharp contrast to the friends of Job who, in the face of his depression, challenged his wisdom and treated him with disrespect and verbal abuse.

> Job replied: "I have heard many things like these; miserable comforters are you all! Will your long-winded speeches never end? What ails you that you keep on arguing? I also could speak like you, if you were in my place; I could make fine speeches against you and shake my head at you. But my mouth would encourage you; comfort from my lips would bring you relief" (Job 16:1-5).

I have found encouragement to be one of the most needed elements in relationships. God has given abilities and gifts to all believers; yet we often focus on weaknesses rather than those abilities. Is it any wonder people fail when their friends only point at weaknesses and not at the competencies God has given them? My wife is a great encourager of me and of others. God uses her to believe in people and to point out their abilities until they can believe in themselves. This is a great gift of caring for those who may be troubled.

A fifth step in assisting someone who is needy: Help them focus on progress. Naomi's progress toward wholeness can be seen by some of her later statements. "How did it go, my daughter?" (Ruth 3:16). These are not the words of a depressed woman.

Persons who are depressed show little awareness of daily activities and even less concern for others. Naomi's words at this point in the narrative were active and interested. Ruth's sharing of the generosity of Boaz ignited her imagination and enabled her once again to encounter life.

Our task, like that of Ruth, is to help the needy person see the results of God at work. This is true for one needing support as well as for a depressed person. Support does more than sympathize. True caring demands that we point them to a God who cares. Caution should be given at this point. Do not rely strictly on telling as a means of helping people realize the working of God in their lives. Denial usually results. By asking questions or referring to what others have discovered for themselves, one can effectively point people to God. Because of Ruth's close involvement with Naomi she was able to bring her to a point of tasting victory instead of bitterness. Ruth led her by positive encouragement, not lectures.

Finally, Ruth helped Naomi experience God's great blessing on them both. She presented her with a grandson. God was still dealing with Naomi's depression, helping her to see His great faithfulness. Her friends declared God's goodness.

> "Praise be to the LORD, who this day has not left you without a kinsman-redeemer. May he become famous throughout Israel! He will renew your life and sustain you in your old age. For your daughter-in-law, who loves you and who is better to you than seven sons, has given him birth" (Ruth 4:14, 15).

Two things raise our interest from this passage. Naomi's friends began to recognize Ruth's efforts. Second, Naomi's friends helped at this point even though there was little evidence to show they had helped or were concerned about her earlier.

The caring process bore real fruit at this point. Naomi had been strengthened and restored. Ruth was faithful. Her reward? She saw Naomi's recovery and was blessed by God herself. Ruth stayed with Naomi, acted on her behalf, showed respect for her, encouraged her competency, focused upon progress, and finally—reminded her of God's faithfulness. You, the reader, can use this single series of actions to care for your friends or family members in whatever stage of life they might be. The steps may also serve as a guide for dealing with your own needs.

We have emphasized that for many persons, caring is a lost treasure. For still others, it is undiscovered. If I were to invite you to cruise the Caribbean Sea in search of sunken ships loaded with jewels and gold, you would do so with excitement. The excitement would build as I unfolded a wrinkled map that other seekers had used, and used successfully. You would think of your family and friends, and all who could find the riches with you. . . .

We recognize that there is no perfect treasure map. The ideas which follow are not quick solutions. You will not get wealthy overnight. However, fellow treasure seekers have tried some of these ideas and have staked their claim on a life filled with more caring for others. These people are becoming wealthy; not financially, but emotionally and spiritually.

It is my sincere desire that you will invest the time and effort necessary to find the lost treasure. As you learn to care more effectively for family members and friends, you will experience feelings that the shepherd felt when he found the lost sheep, or the housewife when she found the lost coin.

> "Or suppose a woman has ten silver coins and loses one. Does she not light a lamp, sweep the house and search carefully until she finds it? And when she finds it, she calls her friends and neighbors together and says, 'Rejoice with me; I have found my lost coin' " (Luke 15:8-9).

2

Finding the Right Model to Follow

Looking unto Jesus

CARING IS A SKILL that you must learn. It is not automatic. As you will see in chapter 3, it isn't even natural.

We learn caring in the way other skills are learned. First, we observe someone who knows how to care. Then we try it on our own. Without a doubt, we'll probably make lots of mistakes. However, if we observe a successful caring model, we will be able to stay on the right track.

In the first chapter, we observed three separate people model the caring process—an adult, a friend, a daughter-in-law. In this chapter, we will look at one Person, Jesus Christ. How was He able to care for an abundance of people who had such a wide range of needs?

Understanding the Needs of People

As we read the gospels, it is fascinating to observe the way in which Jesus was always alert to what was happening with the people around Him. He centered on understanding others. That attitude sharply contrasts with the self-centeredness portrayed by His disciples (then and now). People felt cared for because Jesus' sensitivity went beyond the obvious. Chapter 4 focuses on this concern; it offers specific help in understanding the needs of others.

Accepting People Where They Are

In addition to understanding needs, Jesus had the rare ability to accept people where they were. He was a carer first, not a corrector. Many people learn how to correct, as a parent would correct a child. But they never learn to care.

Jesus accepted Thomas right where he was—in the middle of his doubt. When Jesus appeared to the disciples, He went directly to Thomas. Jesus greeted him and gave him reason to believe. Then, and only then, did He remind him to replace doubting with believing. Thomas was not humiliated. Christ had not berated him. The Lord ministered and then admonished, with care. And Thomas responded with warmth and worship.

I find husbands and wives could take their cue from Jesus about avoiding a corrective or critical spirit. Consider how little you feel someone cares for you when he corrects you without considering your needs. Jesus recognized that. Jesus knew Thomas needed to be shown first; then he could be encouraged to believe.

> Now Thomas (called Didymus), one of the Twelve, was not with the disciples when Jesus came. When the other disciples told him that they had seen the Lord, he declared, "Unless I see the nail marks in his hands and put my finger where the nails were, and put my hand into his side, I will not believe it."
>
> A week later his disciples were in the house again, and Thomas was with them. Though the doors were locked, Jesus came and stood among them and said, "Peace be with you!" Then he said to Thomas, "Put your finger here; see my hands. Reach out your hand and put it into my side. Stop doubting and believe."
>
> Thomas said to him, "My Lord and my God!" (John 20:24-28).

The most tragic relationship Jesus ever entered into is yet another beautiful example of Jesus accepting people where they were. Jesus knew that Judas was going to betray Him, yet He did not exclude him from the passover feast. In fact, Judas most likely had a place next to Jesus, because they dipped in the bowl of food together. When Judas asked Jesus about the betrayal, Jesus did not shy away from telling him the truth. He told of Judas's future without berating him or embarrassing him before the others, however. And at the peak of personal disappointment, when Judas betrayed Him with a kiss, Jesus accepted his action and called Judas friend, or comrade. I believe that Jesus' caring acts for Judas enabled him to acknowledge his sin and try to reverse his action. Unfortunately, it was too late to stop the machinery of death.

> When Judas, who had betrayed him, saw that Jesus was condemned, he was seized with remorse and returned the thirty silver coins to the chief priests and the elders. "I have sinned," he said, "for I have betrayed innocent blood."
> "What is that to us?" they replied. "That's your responsibility."
> So Judas threw the money into the temple and left. Then he went away and hanged himself (Matthew 27:3-5).

John Powell provides a good description of accepting people where they are.

> The essential message of unconditional love is one of liberation: You can be whoever you are, express all your thoughts and feelings with absolute confidence. You do not have to be fearful that love will be taken away. You will not be punished for your openness or honesty. There is no admission price to my love, no rental fees or installment payments to be made. There may be days when disagreements and disturbing emotions may come between us. There may be times when psychological or physical miles may lie between us. But I have given you the word of my commitment. I have set my life on a course. I will not go back on my word to you. So feel free to be yourself, to tell me of your negative and positive reactions, of your warm and cold feelings. I cannot always predict my reactions or guarantee my strength, but one thing I do know and I do want you to know: I will not reject you! I am committed to your growth and happiness. I will always love you.[1]

Accepting the uncertainty of a Thomas and the rejection of a Judas makes Jesus a model for learning how to accept those close to us. Watch the way you interact. Do you show acceptance or correction? If you find that you spend more time correcting than accepting, you can change. You can reverse that process. You will have to guard your tongue for a while. But diligence will see you through the course of breaking the old habit and learning a new one.

Jill and Jim have started down this road of learning. Both need acceptance badly; yet all they seem to offer each other is correction. They will learn to care if they begin accepting the other right where he or she is. The hindrance they must overcome is the temptation to reach out only after the other person has made the first move. Caring in an accepting, unconditional way is a gift, not a good bartered. Powell writes further about loving by accepting.

> The gift of my love means this: I want to share with you whatever I have that is good. You did not win a contest or prove yourself worthy of this gift. It is not a question of deserving my love. I have no delusions that either of us is the best person in the world. I do not even suppose that, of all the available persons, we are the most compatible. I am sure that somewhere there is someone who would be "better" for you or for me. All that is really not to the point. The point is that I have chosen to give you my gift of love and you have chosen to love me. This is the only soil in which love can possibly grow. "We're gonna make it together!"[2]

Extending Mercy

Mercy is an elegant theme found in the beatitudes of the Gospel of Matthew. Matthew 5:7 reads, "Blessed are the merciful, for they will be shown mercy." What does it mean to extend mercy to another? Is extending mercy a way to care for people today?

The word for mercy used in this passage means to have compassion. It is a word of action and reaction. Having compassion is not a passive act, a sweet sentiment given in a quiet atmosphere. Matthew records many times in which others criticized Jesus for his behavior. He gave compassion in return. In Matthew 9:11 His disciples were asked, "Why does your teacher eat with tax collectors and 'sinners'?" In Matthew 12:2 the Pharisees said, "Look! Your disciples are doing what is unlawful on the Sabbath." Jesus responded to both of these instances by quoting Hosea 6:6: "For I desire mercy, not sacrifice, and acknowledgment of God rather than burnt offerings."

There is a principle of mercy here: People are more important than procedure. Grace is more important than legalism. I am merciful when I can compassionately give people what they need, rather than what they deserve.

During His ministry, Jesus was often followed by people who sought either food or healing. Jesus' disciples often grew tired of "tag-alongs" and tried to get Him to send them away. Jesus invariably refused because He was sensitive to their needs and to their cries for mercy. The disciples would gladly have been rid of the Canaanite woman. Not Jesus.

> Leaving that place, Jesus withdrew to the region of Tyre and Sidon. A Canaanite woman from that vicinity came to him, crying out, "Lord, Son of David, have mercy on me! My daughter is suffering terribly from demon-possession."
>
> Jesus did not answer a word. So his disciples came to him and urged him, "Send her away, for she keeps crying out after us."
>
> He answered, "I was sent only to the lost sheep of Israel."
>
> The woman came and knelt before him. "Lord, help me!" she said.
>
> He replied, "It is not right to take the children's bread and toss it to their dogs."
>
> "Yes, Lord," she said, "but even the dogs eat the crumbs that fall from their masters' table."
>
> Then Jesus answered, "Woman, you have great faith! Your request is granted." And her daughter was healed from that very hour (Matthew 15:21-28).

The woman in this story was not a chosen one. She was an outcast, a Canaanite. Jesus used this part of her background to get her to express her faith. Notice His responses before she verbalized her faith. What may seem harsh in reality was a way of helping her understand herself and how He could meet her needs. He didn't rub her nose in her questionable heritage or in her personal sin. He showed mercy.

Showing compassion to the Canaanite woman is directly opposite to the way I function when I am not in a caring mood. I tend to play both judge and jury without really caring for the person. When I argue specifics with someone, I am not being merciful—I am trying to win. I am not filled with compassion. I am filled with competitiveness. Do you ever forget what originally started an argument and still remember every detail of the battle? That is the attitude I'm talking about. It is what psychologists call playing the game.

"Now I've got you" is the motto. It is a deadly, non-caring game which doesn't line up very well with the way Scripture teaches us to live.

Do you ever watch people with the secret hope that they will make a slip? If so, you have a great opportunity to grow. Allowing God to change this attitude into an attitude of love and mercy may change your entire life and relationships. Paul wrote, ". . . it (love) keeps no record of wrongs. Love does not delight in evil but rejoices with the truth. It always protects, always trusts, always hopes, always perseveres" (1 Corinthians 13:5b-7).

If you want to show mercy, you have to give up the tendency to make people pay for their sins. This harsh attitude doesn't make you feel any better. And it does absolutely nothing for the person who needs your caring. I will be eternally grateful to God for giving me a father who held me responsible for my actions but did not punish me for the sake of punishment. I needed his mercy and knew that his forgiveness was greater than my sin. I felt he cared for me, not just about what I had done.

Suppose you are caught up in this area of calling people to account. You can do something about it. Don't simply beat yourself over the head while demoting yourself with admissions such as "That is just the way I am." When you respond harshly and realize it, go back to the person and acknowledge your mistake. After apologizing, you can start over and say what you would have liked to have said. It will be a pleasant experience for both of you.

One evening Sandy, my wife, criticized me severely for breaking a promise I had made. She did not stop at just telling me what I had done wrong. She rehearsed my error a couple of times.

I began to play my game of hurt child; this meant that I wasn't about to move closer to her. After a period of time, she came back to me and asked if we could talk. We did talk and healing took place. She told me that she had been hurt and disappointed, but she had not really handled the situation the way she wanted to.

"I wanted you to take me seriously," she said, "but I really didn't want to hurt you in the way that I did. I wish I could have just shared the concerns without all the jabs I gave you."

Sandy's courageous act—she had to approach someone who can get nasty when he's hurt—opened up the door for us to return to mercy. I apologized for my lack of responsibility, and we talked about how we wanted to be able to handle the next crisis. When it was all over we each felt deeply cared for by the other. The beatitude had become true in our experience. We had each given and received mercy.

When I read the gospels, sometimes I think that Jesus' favorite phrase was "Go and sin no more." He loved to give mercy. It was and is a way of life for Him. We, too, can be merciful because of Him.

Being Tough but Tender

One of my friends described a mutual friend of ours as a marshmallow with a pit. He went on to explain: "He is soft and tender, but if you bite down on him, you may break a tooth."

In a way, Jesus is like that. He is compassionate, tender, full of mercy, slow to anger, and yet principled and capable of holding people responsible. Jesus is no pushover; He is not wishy-washy. You know it when He cares for you.

In John 21 there is a beautiful story of Jesus reinstating Peter after Peter had denied Him at the time of His arrest, trial, and sentencing. Peter was an arrogant man, and the days of personal shame following the death of Jesus must have been the toughest days of his life. Can you imagine living with these haunting words echoing in your mind: "Even if all fall away on account of you, I never will. . . ." "Even if I have to die with you, I will never disown you" (Matthew 26:33b, 35a).

Peter was broken. You and I fail, and break in the aftermath. Jesus does not leave us in our brokenness, though. He cares enough to initiate putting the pieces back together. This is where tender and tough often come together.

After Jesus had met the physical needs of the disciples—showing them where to catch fish, serving them breakfast—He turned to Peter's needs.

> When they had finished eating, Jesus said to Simon Peter, "Simon son of John, do you truly love me more than these?"

> "Yes, Lord," he said, "you know that I love you."
> Jesus said, "Feed my lambs."
> Again Jesus said, "Simon son of John, do you truly love me?"
> He answered, "Yes, Lord, you know that I love you."
> Jesus said, "Take care of my sheep."
> The third time he said to him, "Simon son of John, do you love me?"
> Peter was hurt because Jesus asked him the third time, "Do you love me?" He said, "Lord, you know all things; you know that I love you."
> Jesus said, "Feed my sheep" (John 21:15-17).

Are you tough (punitive) or too tender (no backbone) in your caring? You cannot truly care unless you can tell it like it is. At the same time, you are not really caring if you let people off the hook and allow them to be less than they can be.

Constructive love is the key. Jesus never stopped loving. He refused to become bitter even in the face of flagrant denial by the one who loved him. He joined together assertiveness and aggressiveness in the right proportions.

> The person who carries a desire for self-expression to the extreme of aggressive behavior accomplishes goals usually at the expense of others. Although frequently self-enhancing and expressive of feelings in the situation, aggressive behavior hurts others in the process by making choices for them, and minimizing their worth as persons. Aggressive behavior commonly results in a "put down" of the receiver. Rights denied, she or he feels hurt, defensive, and humiliated. His or her goals in the situation, of course, are not achieved. The aggressive person may achieve goals, but may also generate hatred and frustration which may later return as vengeance.
> In contrast, appropriately assertive behavior in the same situation would be self-enhancing for the actor, an honest expression of feelings, and usually achieve goals. . . . In the case of assertion, neither person is hurt, and unless their goal achievement is mutually exclusive, both may succeed.[3]

The tender-tough connection can make the difference in two typical caring relationships, marriage and friendship.

Ron is usually very supportive of Jane. He is quick to tell her what she does right and how much her life contributes to his. Though they are not overtly affectionate in public, their eyes meet often in affectionate looks. Jane responds by giving to Ron. Neither wants to be superior. They have learned that life is too short for that type of pettiness.

Now for the tough part. It comes when they disagree. Each will stand up to the other, but each listens carefully to what the other person has to say. They respect each other's toughness, and because of that respect, they usually carve out decisions which represent the best thinking of both. Their children respect them, for they have seen both the tenderness and the toughness. They have learned that toughness doesn't have to have thorns.

I have seen the tender-tough connection in my friendship with a very caring individual, Dr. DeLoss Friesen. Uncle Friesen (as my children call him) and I cherish twenty years of friendship. We studied together in graduate school and wrote our dissertations together. We still spend time together sharing ideas and activities.

This isn't what makes our friendship unusual. What makes it unusual is the toughness.

We each have called and confronted the other when we have seen patterns of thought or behavior which were off target. I remember a morning call in which he said, "I have been thinking about what you told me yesterday, and I think you are in over your head. I am willing to talk the situation through with you if you have the time." He didn't force me but he stood by. He was right. I wasn't seeing the particular situation clearly. I was too involved in the decision to see all the variables. Without condemning me he cared by asking me to take a second look. Our friendship is tough enough to confront—tender enough to support and build up. Augsburger refers to this type of person as a peacemaker.

> Wanted:
> Peacemakers.
> Caring people who dare to be present with people when they are hurting and stand with people where they are hurting.
> Peacemaking begins by truly being there for others.[4]

Being Spiritual and Practical

Some Christians are said to be so spiritually minded that they are not of any earthly good. In other words, they don't have time to care because they have their heads in the clouds.

Jesus was certainly not guilty of cloud sitting. He always seemed busy with practical matters like alleviating pain, feeding people, and holding children on His lap. His care and concern reached to practical matters like a cup of cold water for children (Matthew 10:42). He cared when people were hungry or thirsty. He had a unique ability to see people both as souls to be saved and persons to be served.

When Jesus' mother told Him of the need for more wine at the wedding feast, He did more than fill the need; He brought out the best wine.

> Jesus said to the servants, "Fill the jars with water"; so they filled them to the brim.
> Then he told them, "Now draw some out and take it to the master of the banquet."
> They did so, and the master of the banquet tasted the water that had been turned into wine. He did not realize where it had come from, though the servants who had drawn the water knew. Then he called the bridegroom aside and said, "Everyone brings out the choice wine first and then the cheaper wine after the guests have had too much to drink; but you have saved the best till now."
> This, the first of his miraculous signs, Jesus performed in Cana of Galilee. He thus revealed his glory, and his disciples put their faith in him (John 2:7-11).

Jesus cared for people by giving them the best. He knew about quality of life.

> "Which of you fathers, if your son asks for a fish, will give him a snake instead? Or if he asks for an egg, will give him a scorpion? If you then, though you are evil, know how to give good gifts to your children, how much more will your Father in heaven give the Holy Spirit to those who ask him!" (Luke 11:11-13).

Jesus emphasized the giving of good gifts. Nothing less can truly show the glory of God. In our caring relationships, we need to give people the best that we have, not just the left-overs.

If I ask my wife for a date, I don't have to spend a lot of money on her; but I do need to give her the best that I have. I can leave my crabbiness at the office. I can relax and focus on her beauty. I can listen and laugh and love. I don't have to give up my spirituality to do that. In fact, the more spiritual I am the more practical I become in my ability to care for those around me. This kind of practical caring is the Spirit's fruit.

> But the fruit of the Spirit is love, joy, peace, patience, kindness, goodness, faithfulness, gentleness and self-control. Against such things there is no law (Galatians 5:22-23).

Crying with Those Who Cry

Giving comfort is one of the hallmarks of caring. Everyone needs it at one time or another, and yet it is one of the most difficult things to give.

When my wife or my children are hurting, I don't always know how to respond. I feel so inadequate. I know they need me, but I don't know how to be the person they need.

I experienced the inadequacy of how to comfort quite vividly following my cousin's death. Asked to conduct the memorial service, I also had the privilege of ministering to the grieving family. It was a privilege I didn't know how to claim. Sandy and I stood frozen at the door of the funeral home. We knew we had to go in, but we did not know what to say or do for our relatives gathered to view the body and mourn. We prayed for guidance, and symbolically I rolled up my sleeves and stepped through the door. "God," I said, "I can't do it. You do it for me."

I found myself holding, patting, praying, crying, and listening, sharing my own hurt with the family and even respectfully laughing over a shared memory. I learned from that experience that the key was willingness. Sometimes the only way to do something is to do it. I wondered how Jesus felt when He, too, comforted His friends and family following the death of Lazarus.

> When Jesus saw her weeping, and the Jews who had come along with her also weeping, he was deeply moved in spirit and troubled. "Where have you laid him?" he asked.

> "Come and see, Lord," they replied.
> Jesus wept.
> Then the Jews said, "See how he loved him!"
> But some of them said, "Could not he who opened the eyes of the blind man have kept this man from dying?"
> Jesus, once more deeply moved, came to the tomb. It was a cave with a stone laid across the entrance. "Take away the stone," he said.
> "But, Lord," said Martha, the sister of the dead man, "by this time there is a bad odor, for he has been there four days."
> Then Jesus said, "Did I not tell you that if you believed, you would see the glory of God?" (John 11:33-40).

Two comfort characteristics stand out in this passage. Jesus shared His feelings. He did not try to hide them or cover them up. Second, even in the midst of sorrow, he maintained an attitude of hope. Conveyance of feelings and of hope are both important parts of caring for others when you face grief together.

There is no right way to feel. Just being with the person is a sign of care. As I studied John 11, I realized that Jesus risked His very life in order to care for Mary and Martha and the others during this time (see John 11:8). He risked His life just to be there, since He could have healed at a distance (see John 4:43-53). He cared enough to go.

Rejoicing with Those Who Rejoice

So much of the biblical account of the life of Jesus reads in a serious tone. It is hard to get a rounded picture of how He related to happy situations. I have a suspicion that He was enthusiastic and joyful throughout life, even in the face of His impending death.

Traditionally we picture a joyful meeting between Zaccheus and Jesus. Jesus singled Zaccheus out and invited Himself to his home for a meal. This wasn't the socially acceptable thing to do. Grumbling may have erupted from the Pharisees and the disciples or both. For Jesus and Zaccheus, though, this was a very special time, a joyful time. Notice their crisp dialogue.

> But Zacchaeus stood up and said to the Lord, "Look,
> Lord! Here and now I give half of my possessions to the
> poor, and if I have cheated anybody out of anything, I
> will pay back four times the amount."
>   Jesus said to him, "Today salvation has come to this
> house, because this man, too, is a son of Abraham. For
> the Son of Man came to seek and to save what was lost"
> (Luke 19:8-10).

Jesus was factual and to the point, but He was not a
"heavy" or a "wet blanket." He liked life, and His attitude
stirred life in others. What is an abundant life if it isn't a life of
rejoicing?

If you want to be a caring person, allow yourself to get excited about the good things that are happening in the lives of
those for whom you care. Take time to laugh and play. Take
time to feel the rain and smell the flowers with those you
love. We spend far too much time controlling people's joy
and so little time encouraging joy. Then we puzzle over why
life and people are dull.

My personal mascot is the dolphin. People wonder why. I
adopted the dolphin when I read that these mammals are intelligent, trusting, and playful. I can't do much to change my
intelligence quotient, but I can strive to be trusting and playful. The brass dolphin on my desk reminds me to care for
others in this way. Take the risk of being enthusiastic with
those for whom you care. It may change your entire life.

Being Process-, Not Product-Oriented

Our production-oriented society alters our whole orientation toward life. If I ask you who you are, you will probably
tell what you do or what you make. You say, "I'm a housewife," or "I'm an engineer." Rarely do I respond to such a
question by saying, "I'm one of God's loved ones," or "I'm
Sandy Wilson's husband." In identifying myself, I trade off
the more important things in life—relationships—in favor of
some product which I produce.

Too many people live performance-based lives; they never
feel good about themselves because they do not produce
enough. Jesus acted against this error of thinking in His relationship with His friends, Mary and Martha. He and Mary
sat and talked with one another, caring for each other by

spending time together. Now Martha was product-oriented. She couldn't sit by when things needed to be done.

> As Jesus and his disciples were on their way, he came to a village where a woman named Martha opened her home to him. She had a sister called Mary, who sat at the Lord's feet listening to what he said. But Martha was distracted by all the preparations that had to be made. She came to him and asked, "Lord, don't you care that my sister has left me to do the work by myself? Tell her to help me!"
>
> "Martha, Martha," the Lord answered, "you are worried and upset about many things, but only one thing is needed. Mary has chosen what is better, and it will not be taken away from her" (Luke 10:38-42).

Jesus was not implying that working in the kitchen or the garage is not important. He was saying that doing is not more important than being—or being with. We need to retrain ourselves so that we do value being with God, our family members, and our friends. People really feel cared for when time is spent with them and on them.

What happens when you are oriented toward a product and your friend or spouse may be process-oriented? Confusion! Disappointment! Conflict!

If you want to care for the other person, you need to be willing to change to the other person's orientation. We have talked about changing to a process-orientation. Yet if your friend is product-oriented, you may need to be with him or her while he or she is producing a product. If your friend is process-oriented, you may need to go just to spend time with that friend and give up your own need to produce.

You communicate care and build relationships when you are willing to reach out to the other person in the way that is safest for them. I'm sure that Jesus would have been willing to visit and help in the kitchen with Martha while she produced the meal had the time with Mary not been the more needed example.

Caring is a process. It is hard to see the results at first. We need to follow the example of Jesus and stay with the process whether we see a product or not . . . ever. The nature of caring determines this unconditional approach. Tournier's analysis of the current status of understanding could easily be applied to the process of caring.

We must be reminded that the first condition for mutual understanding is the desire for, the seeking after, and the willing of that understanding. Such a statement may appear very commonplace. Nevertheless, this basic attitude toward understanding others is far rarer than we think. Listen to all the conversations of our world, those between nations as well as those between couples. They are for the most part dialogues of the deaf. Each one speaks primarily in order to set forth his own ideas, in order to justify himself, in order to enhance himself and to accuse others. Exceedingly few exchanges of viewpoints manifest a real desire to understand the other person.[5]

Personalizing the Model

We have looked at Jesus as a model for caring in several different situations, with several different people. In reality, we have barely scratched the surface of Christ's care-filled life. The more you learn *of* Jesus, the more you can learn *from* Him.

May I suggest that if you want to become a caring person, you need to read over and over again the accounts of Jesus interacting with people. They may not all relate to you in specific circumstances, but chances are good that if you continue to learn from His story you will find yourself changing in some very positive ways. You are not perfect and you cannot care in a perfect way. You *can* begin to take baby steps, though. Those first efforts will be followed by stronger steps as you continue to watch Him, your model.

Chapter 2, Notes

[1]John Powell, *Unconditional Love* (Niles, Ill.: Argus Communications, 1978), pp. 66, 67.

[2]Ibid., pp. 65-66.

[3]Robert E. Alberti, Ph.D. and Michael L. Emmons, Ph.D. *Your Perfect Right* (San Luis Obispo, Calif.: Impact, 1974), pp. 10-12.

[4]David Augsburger, *Caring Enough to Confront* (Ventura, Calif.: Regal Books, 1981), p. 127.

[5]Paul Tournier, *To Understand Each Other* (Richmond, Va.: John Knox Press, 1967), pp. 8, 9.

3

Developing a Caring Attitude

Caring is not natural—
allow God to work in you

I HAVE TAKEN THE approach when working with people that people can care for others if they know how. Thus, chapter 2 two emphasized some of Jesus' caring skills that we can learn. We can learn and we can care, *if we want to*. That is the subject of this chapter: getting to the point when I want to care. Just as Jesus is my model for caring behavior, I find that He is also my model for a caring attitude. The challenge of Philippians 2 confronts me all the time.

> Your attitude should be the same as that of Christ Jesus: Who, being in very nature God, did not consider equality with God something to be grasped, but made himself nothing, taking the very nature of a servant, being made in human likeness. And being found in appearance as a man, he humbled himself and became obedient to death—even death on a cross! (Philippians 2:5-8).

Jesus here shows the essence of selflessness. As I look at people around me, I see that selflessness and caring go together. You must give up some of yourself in order to be able to care for another. When I say that selflessness and caring walk hand in hand, I am not talking about lack of self-love. I must love myself if I want to care, but I dare not be self-centered if I want to care.

Let me restate the path for developing a caring attitude. I want to develop an attitude of caring. So I will allow God to change the focus of my life. The needs of others can now become as important as my own needs. A prime biblical example of this change charges husbands to have such an attitude in Ephesians 5:28-29. To care for one's wife—or another person—is to be willing to nourish or cherish the other person as you nourish or cherish yourself.

This remarkable challenge cannot be met without the intervention of God and some self-discipline of our own.

Understanding the Process of Attitude Change

Most people discover that attitude change is very difficult. "I'd like to change, but I'm pretty set in my ways" is a typical challenge made to the idea of change. If you sit in a corner and listen to Christian people talk about the change process, you will come up with a lot of different responses. One person may say, "It is impossible. You are the way you are and there isn't really anything you can do about it." Another person may say, "Don't worry about it. God will change you when He wants you changed." Other people fall in the middle. They believe change occurs when God works *and* when we work. These people believe that a change in attitude is the result of cooperation between God and us. Yet it is a rare combination of faith and action that allows us to change either our attitudes or our behavior.

In working with people who struggle to learn the caring process, I have noticed a pattern in those individuals who are succeeding. Figure 1 diagrams this pattern.

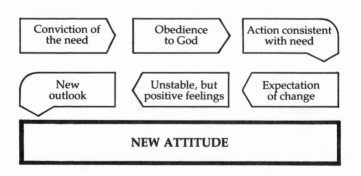

Figure 1: Steps in Attitude Change

Each of these steps deserves a closer look. People often say that if you really wanted to change, you would. It's as simple as that. This is a half-truth. To be ready for change, I must be convicted of the need for a better attitude. In addition, I need a glimpse of the difference a better attitude could make.

Recently I conducted a seminar for men on the topic "Developing Friendships with Family Members." One of the activities I had the men do was to draw a chart of their family. On it they were supposed to show the types of relationships which existed between family members. The men had to examine specifically how close they were emotionally to the other family members. We were looking at connectedness and closeness.

One man summarized his thoughts about the drawing exercise, "When you asked me to do that exercise, I felt everything was fine in my family. By the time I was finished, I realized that four of us were connected to each other and one person—my son—was cut off to the side, all alone." After thinking about the situation for awhile, he said, "I need to find out what is wrong. I don't know what is causing this or allowing this to happen; but I want things to change."

John 16:8 declares that the Counselor, the Holy Spirit, has the responsibility to convict us of "sin and righteousness and judgment." This conviction may come through reading the Bible and helpful books, listening to sermons, talking with your spouse or a friend, or through meditating and praying. How we are convicted doesn't matter. Moving to the second step of attitude change does matter. How will we respond to the conviction? Being convicted is not the same as changing. Being convicted is easier. Many times I have had good intentions, but I have not responded with obedience.

Obedience begins with taking action. Graphically stated, you must put yourself on the line whether you feel like it or not. The hardest part for our friend who wanted to change his attitude and behavior toward his son was to begin that next action step with himself. I'm sure he thought of dozens of reasons why he should start reaching out to that son *the next day*. Unfortunately, things never get done the next day. They only get done *now*. The longer you wait to obey God, the greater the fears about obedience and its costs become.

Fear is the culprit that often steals the desire for a caring attitude in the first place. Fear creates inertia. Not acting creates fear. The only cure for fear is faith and trust that God will guide our steps. First John 4 makes it clear that the love of God is able to drive out fear.

> There is no fear in love. But perfect love drives out fear, because fear has to do with punishment. The man who fears is not made perfect in love.
>   We love because he first loved us. If anyone says, "I love God," yet hates his brother, he is a liar. For anyone who does not love his brother, whom he has seen, cannot love God, whom he has not seen. And he has given us this command: Whoever loves God must also love his brother (1 John 4:18-21).

Release from fear doesn't happen automatically. It happens when we begin to act on the truth, when we love as He loves. Verse 21 implies that in matters of loving others, we are not given an option of holding back our love. The word "must" is used. "Whoever loves God must also love his brother." As we take the step of obeying God by loving others, we can experience God's power in changing our attitudes. The action of loving is consistent with our need to change.

I will never forget standing with a father and his mentally handicapped son at the base of a rugged peak in the mountains of Colorado. The son turned to the father and said, "Will you go up with me, Dad?" Indeed, this was the moment of truth.

The father's face was white with fear. He turned to me searching for an escape. Finally he said, "I think God wants me to do this, but I don't know whether I can."

"We'll pray," I said.

The leader of the hike called people to fall in line and follow him. When they got to the last fifty feet, the father saw he would have to climb the rocks with a rope. He was almost overtaken again. With a burst of courage, he charged to the head of the line with his son and shouted, "We need to do this now!" Both made it to the top. Not without slips and not without doubts. But both made it.

When I joined them at the top, we shared together the gorgeous sixty-mile panorama. The son said, "Thanks, Daddy! Now I won't be afraid to climb trees with my friends." My eyes dampened, and it wasn't because of the bright sun or the wind! This father had been obedient even though he was scared. He took the steps, and God met him there. It was a remarkable example of learning to care. The father later told the group that he felt this experience had begun to change his entire attitude toward his son. Who could doubt it?

The topic of attitudes cannot be separated from that of expectations. In reality, what we expect is often what we experience. If I believe that I cannot deal with a particular person or situation, I will usually have a bad experience. My attitude will become even more negative. On the other hand, if I expect God to work to change my attitude it often will.

Positive action and positive expectation usually go hand in hand as one develops an attitude of caring. If I expect something good to happen, I am less protective and less fearful; this often facilitates the change I would like to see. If you have been praying for a new attitude, expect it to happen. Look for evidence of the change happening, and then act as if the change had taken place already.

You want to be more loving toward your spouse. Act as if your attitude has already changed. Reach out toward your spouse as though God has already rejuvenated and recharged your love for your mate. By the time you have reached out, you may find that He already has changed you.

Debbie was very angry with her husband because he seemed so selfish and uncaring. In the process of discussing her anger, she came to realize that she did not have a caring attitude either. "I don't even know if I love him anymore," she said. Later she admitted, "I do want to do what is right, but I don't know if I care for him. He has hurt me so badly. I'm not sure I can recover." I challenged her to think about what she would do if she did care for him. We made a list. She began to do some of these things, and as she changed her behavior, her attitude changed. "It felt good," she said. "Even when he didn't respond, I knew I was being who God wanted me to be. I need to care because God made me that way."

Debbie's expectation was becoming more and more positive. She opened up to new ways of showing her husband that he was special to her. When he acted like a fool, she was discouraged and even hurt—but not defeated. When he did respond positively, it was like frosting on the cake.

Debbie was at this stage beginning to experience the next step—unstable, but positive feelings. In his intriguing book, *Three Steps Forward, Two Steps Back,* Swindoll points out that personal, spiritual growth is not an even, steady process.

> Growing and learning. That's the Christian life in a nutshell, isn't it? It seems to me that more of us in God's family ought to admit that there are more "growing and learning" days than "great and fantastic" days. And that's nothing to be ashamed of. Growing and learning are healthy, normal experiences. Both have to do with a process . . . and that process is sometimes painful, often slow, and occasionally downright awful! It's like taking three steps forward and two steps back.
>
> Don't misunderstand, Jesus is still Lord, God is still good. The victory is still ours. Nevertheless, life is tough. It's not a Disneyland. Or a rose garden. Or a Cloud Nine delight complete with loud fireworks and big-time tingles. Or daily miracles that make our checkbooks balance and recharge our dead batteries. Such expectations are not only unrealistic, they are unbiblical.[1]

We see this same pattern when God changes our attitudes. Just because you are becoming a caring person doesn't mean that you will be caring all the time. Some days you will blow it completely. The issue is not whether you will fail. You will! The issue is whether you choose to look at your failures or at your successes. If you look at your successes, you will be ready to experience new successes. If you look at your failures, you will be afraid to trust God to give you a new attitude.

Each step that you take toward your goal of becoming a caring person will better prepare you for the next opportunity. Even if you slide back, you will recognize that you did care at least that one time. God did use that experience for you and for your spouse, family member, or friend.

When I took skiing lessons, I felt overwhelmed. I wasn't sure I could do anything right. I just knew I would kill someone (I had the uneasy feeling that the someone might be me). After a little while, I began to see one or two things I was doing right. Of course I fell down a few times. And it hurt!

By the second day of my snow adventures, I felt okay as long as I stayed on the beginner's siope. The problem was my instructor. He had different ideas. "You can't learn any more here," he said. "You have to push yourself." When I started down the intermediate slope, it happened. Just as I feared, I lost control and was heading straight down the hill on a collision course with a fellow student. She screamed—disaster was inevitable! I remembered only one basic maneuver: a snow plow turn. I only turned about one foot, but that was enough to miss my classmate. We both felt relieved—and safe again—and I knew I had learned something.

Even if your attempts to care or your caring attitude get out of control, keep trying. Your feelings may be unstable, but each positive experience gives you another positive on which to build. An attitude of caring is not an all or none proposition, or a once and for all final state. Sometimes I feel more like caring than at others. Other times I care less. But the attitude change continues as I build on those positive results.

You probably heard the phrase, "He is an accident looking for a place to happen." I see myself as a care package looking for a place to be delivered. This is a new outlook. I am focusing on a new style of life and relationships. This new outlook is focused on the command of Paul to the Ephesians.

> Be kind and compassionate to one another, forgiving each other, just as in Christ God forgave you. Be imitators of God, therefore, as dearly loved children and live a life of love, just as Christ loved us and gave himself up for us as a fragrant offering and sacrifice to God (Ephesians 4:32-5:2).

A new outlook gives you an attitude of wanting to be like Jesus in your ability to care. Once this passage sinks in, you may want to go back and reread chapter 2 in this book.

The final step is having the new attitude. Positively identifying when that happens is hard. Usually you just know that you are seeing more needs. Some of the selfish, childish, little things begin to shrink in their importance. This is the process of becoming more like Jesus in our attitudes toward self and others. It is an exciting way to live!

Confronting the Enemies

Although we have made fleeting reference to two of the enemies of attitude change—fear and selfishness—we want to discuss them more fully. In addition, we will look at the problems of a lack of faith and doing things out of spite. Both are contrary to developing a caring attitude.

Consider fear and lack of faith together, because they usually go together. When I am not trusting God to help me to care for others, I am usually afraid to even try caring for them. Likewise, when I am fearful of trying something new, I find it difficult to exercise faith.

These two enemies to a caring attitude can be illustrated by two stories, one from the Bible and one from the experience of a husband and wife who are trying to learn to care.

The Bible story is the parable of the talents which we find in Matthew 25:14-30. Although we don't specifically know what the talents are, I feel safe in assuming they could be relationship talents as well as managerial or physical skills, or money to be invested. Whatever the talents were, the story is clear: Different persons chose to use their talents or opportunities in different ways. Two persons invested them immediately, but the third person "went off, dug a hole in the ground and hid his master's money" (Matthew 25:18). This man undoubtedly didn't feel like he had received much; but the key is that he was afraid to use what he had. Notice what he said:

> Then the man who had received the one talent came. "Master," he said, "I knew that you are a hard man, harvesting where you have not sown and gathering where you have not scattered seed. So I was afraid and went out and hid your talent in the ground. See, here is what belongs to you" (Matthew 25:24-25).

You can see a lack of faith in verse 24. The man's concept of God focused on punishment rather than on God's ability to bless and multiply. In addition, verse 25 shows his fear reaction. He wasn't really trying to live. He was just trying to survive. He hid the talents so that he wouldn't lose them. He was afraid to allow God to develop his potential.

Apply this parable to caring for those around you. It may seem that others know how to say or do the right things. So what is that to you? Is that any reason for you not to exercise the caring muscles that God has given you? I think not! In fact, the more you exercise, the more dramatic will be your growth. As you allow God to orient you toward people and their needs, you will be amazed at yourself.

Don't let these enemies hold you back. God will be with you even when you are fearful. I believe that this biblical principle is true in regard to relationships.

> For whoever wants to save his life will lose it, but whoever loses his life for me will save it (Luke 9:24).

Michael and Lois illustrate how fear can be an enemy of caring. They are married—and want to be. They want to be happy. But each is afraid to trust the other. This blocks the caring attitude. They hold back because they are afraid of doing the wrong thing. Believing that God can and will guide them, even in the way they relate to each other, is hard. They get so worried about the other's response that they become immobilized. What could be a joyful, happy relationship is being choked out by fear of not meeting the other's expectations.

"So what if you don't meet the other person's needs perfectly?" I asked. "What is the worst thing that could happen? Could the feared happening be any worse than the emotional famine you are experiencing now? Could God be any more distant when you step out to try to care for your mate than He seems when you hold back in fear?"

We may hold back because we fear being hurt. It is true that life is risky. In the process of learning to care, Sandy and I have hurt each other. But we have not given up on each other or on our caring God. Above my desk is a framed motto that she gave to me following a particularly difficult time when we tried to care for one another but seemingly missed the mark. The message reads, "Yesterday's hurt is today's understanding, rewoven into tomorrow's love."

The other two enemies of caring that we have identified can also be discussed together. Selfishness and doing things out of spite often occur together.

I have observed many individuals who wanted to be caring people—and indeed thought they were—who refused to use the caring abilities God had given them. Why? Because they felt the other person wanted or demanded it. One man said, "I know she wants me to hold her sometimes, but I just can't bring myself to do it when she wants it." One woman stated, "Why should I care for him when he won't care for me?" As I sat quietly reflecting with her in her sorrow, she continued, "I know I need to be who I am, *regardless* of whether or not he is what I want him to be."

Paul Hauck has underscored the problem of letting spite control your behavior.

> Rather than get involved in power struggles, allow the other person the right to dictate to you. If your mate tells you to stop smoking and you really want to, don't say spitefully that he or she can't make you stop smoking. That's self-evident. Nobody can make you lose weight, clean your house, or stop smoking unless you want to. So stop proving a point that is obvious. It isn't necessary. Simply determine for yourself whether or not this is really what you want to do. If you really want to run your life, then don't let someone else's demands turn you away from what to do. If you want to stop smoking and you do the opposite because you were ordered to stop, then obviously you aren't in control of yourself at all. You are reacting to what someone else said. In effect, your spouse's words are controlling you even though it happens to be in the totally opposite direction from what you wanted. You are not running your life, it is your spouse, or your boss, or whoever.[2]

Dr. Hauck's example of being spiteful happens when someone tells you to do something like stop smoking. You may also be spiteful when someone asks you to do something like care for them in a particular way. Nobody can force you to care. That is evident. On the other hand, if you really care, do not let someone's request for caring detour you in your efforts to become a more caring person.

If spitefulness is hindering you in developing a caring attitude, confess it to God and to the person. This frees you for bigger and better things. Being spiteful reduces your potential. Caring magnifies potential.

What about selfishness, then? Is selfishness always bad?

Selfishness is bad when it hinders you from caring for others. If I care only for myself, and never take the time to give to others, I am not living as God intended. Sometimes I do have to take care of myself in order to have something to give. For example, I need time alone and I need recreation to keep physically and mentally fit. If, however, I only take care of these needs and never stop to realize that Sandy and the children have similar needs, I am not caring for them.

When one person becomes selfish, the spouse or friend often reacts with spitefulness. A vicious, unhealthy cycle develops, and it must be broken for caring to return.

I have become convicted of the selfishness which often prevents me from caring as I would like to for my children. Sometimes I see their needs, but I refuse to meet them because I would have to inconvenience myself (by getting out of my chair, planning another activity, etc.). This is not the attitude of an effective father, and I will lose many of the joys that come from a close relationship with my children.

So I have had to set some goals for myself. Every week I plan to do at least one thing that each child asks me to do which I don't really want to do. I plan to do it for them because I love them. That may not sound like much of a goal, but it is far more satisfying than spending all week just sitting around being selfish. Besides that, our six children make this goal interesting.

You can meet your self-interest without being selfish or spiteful. It is selfish to expect that others will put themselves out for you when you don't try to care for them. Having made that statement about selfishness, let's look at caring. Caring is more than just making excessive sacrifices. Excessive sacrifice may not be caring at all. That's called spoiling the person. Caring is giving and taking. I am free to ask for something because I know I am willing to respond when my friends or family members express their needs. It is a fun way to live. Hauck gives a cute example which illustrates the difference between selfishness and self-interest.

> You lay back on the sofa propped up on a pillow tossing bonbons into your mouth, and give orders to your family to be quiet while they put on your favorite record, make your coffee, and open the window a bit so you can catch the cool breeze. That is being selfish, because you are expecting others to put themselves out exclusively for you with no expectation of your doing something for them. In other words, the selfish person wants something for nothing.
>
> The self-interested person, however, may also want to rest on the sofa, eat bonbons, and want the same services but not actually be a selfish person, for there is every intention of doing something in return for those favors.

> For example, what's selfish about wanting your wife
> to bring you a cup of coffee if you just did the dishes for
> her? And what's selfish about her asking you to do the
> dishes if she cooks the meal? And what's selfish about
> your asking her to open the window and to put on your
> favorite record if you have just come back from picking
> up the dry cleaning?
>
> These are not selfish acts, they're acts of reciprocity,
> acts of payment for services rendered or expected. They
> say that you are important and so is your partner.[3]

Some people react to the concept of reciprocity—giving
and taking—because they feel that it is a selfish type of caring. It is true we shouldn't expect to be paid back for the caring things we do. However, a good caring attitude is rarely
maintained unless you have the freedom to express your
need to the person receiving your care. It is only when you
expect or demand reciprocity that you will find yourself in
trouble. I find nothing unbiblical about the notion "you
scratch my back and I'll scratch yours!" The unbiblical attitude is "I won't scratch your back unless you scratch mine!"

Take the risk of trusting God and trusting people, and
overcome the enemies of care. Look for opportunities to be
caring even in the face of the enemy. If you find yourself caring even when you feel fearful or selfish, you will know even
greater things are possible.

Reframing Your View of Caring

The term "reframing" is used to describe a psychological
therapy technique of seeing events or relationships in a different context. It is like putting a picture in a new frame. If I
am going to develop a caring attitude, I need to reframe my
view of caring and the way in which I view my caring behavior. What are my intentions? Why do I feel some of the
things I feel or do some of the things I do?

I often get caught in the trap of doing things for people,
even caring things, because I feel I have to. This is not the process of becoming more of a caring person.

Reframing might help. What would happen if I looked at
the other person instead of at what I feel I *have* to do?

If I look at my wife, for example, I see a lovely person who
is even more lovely when I am able to provide her with some

refreshing caring. In other words, as I bear some of her burdens or reaffirm some of her strengths, I help her to reach her full potential. Seeing my activities in that framework excites me. I enjoy making her eyes light up. Jesus made an interesting statement about serving others.

> And if anyone gives a cup of cold water to one of these little ones because he is my disciple, I tell you the truth, he will certainly not lose his reward (Matthew 10:42).

I used to be the water boy when I was a kid on the farm. At times I hated the job. It was almost half a mile from our house to the far field, and every time I had to make a trip, it seemed as though the workers were at the farthest point. I never thought of my job as bringing refreshment to people. I only thought of the heavy water and the dry, hot path.

Recently when I read the statement of Jesus from Matthew, I reframed a lot of my caring behavior. I don't have to carry water. I get to refresh. I get to carry life and vitality to those I love. That is exciting! No wonder Jesus said, "You won't lose your reward." The thought of getting to refresh someone you love is in and of itself a tremendous reward.

When our good friends, Arlis and Lyman, come to visit us, Arlis brings her outstanding cookies and bread. When she gives them to us, I can see her eyes light up. She doesn't have to make goodies. She gets to refresh us by making goodies.

The same principle can apply to other caring tasks, such as listening. Listening is hard work. But if you listen to refresh or to help purify the person's thoughts, you will listen with new purpose. You get to serve the person rather than feel that you have an obligation, a boring obligation.

The key to reframing is to keep your focus on the person. Look for opportunities to refresh others. It is a much better option than wallowing in the self-pity that often accompanies many of our relationships. "What can I do to help?" is one of the most psychologically rejuvenating questions you can ask. A noted psychiatrist was asked what he would do if he woke up one morning and discovered that he was terribly depressed. He surprised his audience by saying, "I wouldn't look for a therapist. I would look for someone who needed my help." In other words, he would reframe his experience. He would take himself from the place of self-pity to the place of feeling useful.

Reframing is a skill. It is a skill that makes attitude change possible. If you have a bad attitude about a situation, ask yourself what you are currently telling yourself about the situation. What is your current frame? Write down your answer. Then ask yourself, "What are some other things I could say or ways I could look at the situation?"

Look for better ways to view the circumstances. Write down your answers and again choose the best approach for you. Then practice looking at life through the new frame. When you slip back into the old frame, bring yourself back. Seeing things through the new frame eventually will become very reinforcing and you will find yourself with a new attitude and a new healthy habit. A habit of caring.

Remember, attitude change is a new continuum. No one is perfect. No one cares all the time. You will not care every minute. The real issue is wanting to care more today than you cared yesterday. This is what is called a continuum.

Caring is a continuous process that proceeds from less to more. As you progress, look back and thank God that He has been faithful and He is teaching you to be more like He wants you to be. That act of worship itself will help give you more of a caring attitude.

Chapter 3, Notes

[1]Charles Swindoll, *Three Steps Forward, Two Steps Back* (Nashville: Nelson, 1980), pp. 17, 18.

[2]Paul Hauck, *How to Do What You Want to Do* (Philadelphia: Westminster Press, 1976), p. 32.

[3]Hauck, *How to Stand Up for Yourself* (Philadelphia: Westminster Press, 1979), p. 67.

4

Understanding the Needs of Others

All people are
not like me

WHEN I THINK OF human needs I immediately think of David (and the other psalmists) and how he openly discussed his needs in the Psalms. There is little pretense with David. He brings it all up front. At least in his talks with God, he didn't leave any concerns unstated. If we can categorize needs (as we will later), David didn't leave any categories uncovered. He felt deeply; and he was very open about those feelings.

The Psalms spill over with David's expression of his humanness and his needs as a person. He and the other psalm writers expressed all the needs that modern psychology conceptualizes. There is definite similarity in the needs expressed in Scripture and in the work of Dr. Abraham Maslow, who was a pioneer in the scientific study of needs.

Maslow talked about psychological needs. David spoke prophetically of the physical needs of Christ, the Messiah.

> I am poured out like water, and all my bones are out of joint. My heart has turned to wax; it has melted away within me. My strength is dried up like a potsherd, and my tongue sticks to the roof of my mouth; you lay me in the dust of death. Dogs have surrounded me; a band of evil men has encircled me, they have pierced my hands and my feet. I can count all my bones; people stare and gloat over me. They divide my garments among them and cast lots for my clothing (Psalm 22:14-18).

Maslow talked about safety needs. David was concerned about personal safety.

> O LORD, how many are my foes! How many rise up against me! Many are saying of me, "God will not deliver him."
>
> But you are a shield around me, O LORD, my Glorious One, who lifts up my head. To the LORD I cry aloud, and he answers me from his holy hill (Psalm 3:1-4).

Maslow talked about a need for loving and belonging. The psalmist described the love and the care of the Lord.

> I will sing of the love of the LORD forever; with my mouth I will make your faithfulness known through all generations. I will declare that your love stands firm forever, that you established your faithfulness in heaven itself.
>
> You said, "I have made a covenant with my chosen one, I have sworn to David my servant, 'I will establish your line forever and make your throne firm through all generations'" (Psalm 89:1-4).

Maslow talked of a need for self-esteem. The psalmist spoke about this in Psalm 118.

> The LORD is with me; I will not be afraid. What can man do to me? The LORD is with me; he is my helper. I will look in triumph on my enemies.
>
> It is better to take refuge in the LORD than to trust in man. It is better to take refuge in the LORD than to trust in princes (Psalm 118:6-9).

Maslow talked of self-actualization as the process of reaching your full potential. Listen to David's words one more time.

> I praise you because I am fearfully and wonderfully made; your works are wonderful, I know that full well (Psalm 139:14).

In reading Maslow's list and in reading the Psalms, the breadth of human need comes into full view. The vacuum is so great you wonder if it could ever be filled.

In dealing with my friends and family, I could look at their need list and reel back from its size, overwhelmed and frustrated by my limitations. God does not expect me to meet every need, though. Only He can do that! What He does expect is that I will be open to seeing and addressing the needs which I am able to meet. My abilities and talents do limit my energies in certain directions. Other Christians can care for the needs my talents can't reach. The discussion of spiritual gifts contained in 1 Corinthians 12 and its analogy of a body applies here. We are not all the same parts and therefore cannot all meet the same needs. But together we can care for the needs that collect in our daily lives.

> As it is, there are many parts, but one body.
> The eye cannot say to the hand, "I don't need you!" And the head cannot say to the feet, "I don't need you!" On the contrary, those parts of the body that seem to be weaker are indispensable, and the parts that we think are less honorable we treat with special honor. And the parts that are unpresentable are treated with special modesty, while our presentable parts need no special treatment. But God has combined the members of the body and has given greater honor to the parts that lacked it, so that there should be no division in the body, but that its parts should have equal concern for each other. If one part suffers, every part suffers with it; if one part is honored, every part rejoices with it (1 Corinthians 12:20-26).

This passage affirms each of us in our talents and abilities, then it instructs us to meet the needs of others God has prepared us to meet. In so doing, God meets the needs of the body. If you do not know what needs you can meet most efficiently, try serving, helping, organizing, or planning for others in need. The results and feedback you get will help you understand yourself better.

Five different types of needs will face you as you attempt to care for others. The categories may be familiar, but let's look specifically to find some new handles for caring.

Physical—Need to Do or Get Things Done

Have you ever been completely covered over by things to do? I'm talking about a day when the more things you do, the more things stack up in front of you to be done. Imagine how you would feel if someone came up to you during one of these times and said, "You look like there is something wrong. Would you like to talk about it?" You would probably blow your cool! You don't need empathy. You need help.

Mothers of young children often feel this way. They can't keep up with all the house chores, and all their husbands seem to want to do is play. Husbands feel this way when they are inundated at work, and there is no one to help pick up the load. Being sensitive to physical needs and stepping forward to help is a very important way to care. As we bear one another's burdens, the needs slacken their grip upon us.

I remember vividly being under pressure to teach a class that I felt unqualified and unprepared to teach. The problem was compounded by a busy schedule that had kept me away from the books. When we returned from our vacation, I had one day to get out in front of the pack of eager students so that I could run for my life. I hurried to the office that morning, determined to put in a full day of study.

It didn't work that way! I was greeted by a host of well-meaning friends who were glad to see me and a mound of papers that needed my attention. By noon I was frantic, and I knew I had to retreat.

Where could I go? Ahh!! My home! My castle! All the way home I took solace in the fact that things would be different. I knew I could do it. All I needed was a little peace and quiet. As I turned into the drive, I was even venturing a smile.

I walked toward my house, and then I saw it! There it was right in my own living room. The mess of the century. Chairs stacked high, curtains down, rugs thrown in piles, and the queen of the castle looking ragged and having a smudge of dirt on her face. I was furious! How could she do this to me? Didn't she know I needed help? Didn't she care?

As I stomped up the path, something got a hold of me. An internal, sensitive, still, small voice. What about her? As I opened the door, I did something absolutely insane. I smiled!

"Hi, sweetie," I said. "It looks like you have your hands full." We kissed without biting and I felt compelled to ask her if I could help.

Apologetically she said, "I'm sorry for the mess, but I was feeling a lot of pressure about having the women here when my house was such a mess." I resisted the temptation to tell her how much I thought she had improved it!

Quickly I changed my clothes and rolled up my sleeves. She gave me some instructions, and I went to work. I finished one task, and she gave me another. I went back for thirds, and she obliged. After the rugs were shaken and back in place she said (I will never forget her words), "You know what I would really like you to do? I would like you to hole up in the bedroom and study for a while. That would make me feel good. I'll keep the kids away from you."

I remember thinking, "Now I know there is a God in heaven and I know He cares." I did study, and I did get ahead of my class. By 9:00 P.M., we were both exhausted, but fulfilled and happy. We enjoyed a cup of coffee together and chatted about the day. What a contrast to the disaster I almost created by reacting to the pressures of my needs instead of considering hers. It also makes a living illustration about caring for others.

We have other physical needs. The need for rest. The need for exercise. The need to learn new skills. The need for physical outlets. The need for sexual expression.

Take a moment to visualize your spouse, your friend, or a family member. Think about the physical demands they face. Think about how you would feel physically if you were them. Now think of something you can do for them when you have an opportunity. As you care in this way, you will begin to understand some of the ways you can care for physical needs. Meeting these needs will help the person have more time to care for themselves in other areas. It may also give them more time to reach back and care for you.

Intellectual—Need to Understand or Know

The human brain is a marvelous machine. Those who use it normally feel good about the experience. When God created Adam and Eve, He gave them a distinct command, a command to the intellect.

> So God created man in his own image, in the image of God he created him; male and female he created them.
> God blessed them and said to them, "Be fruitful and increase in number; fill the earth and subdue it. Rule over the fish of the sea and the birds of the air and over every living creature that moves on the ground" (Genesis 1:27-28).

Man is certainly not physically stronger than all the creatures. So if we are to subdue all, it is going to take more than muscle. When God commands, He equips. Thus, He equipped us with a marvelous advantage—our brain. Poets have written much about a person's pursuit of knowledge and his or her pursuit of wisdom. It is God-implanted and therefore represents a genuine area of human need. The need to think and the need to know are central to the meaning of being a human being.

Solomon recognized man's need for knowledge and sought to channel that need in the right direction.

> Stay away from a foolish man, for you will not find knowledge on his lips (Proverbs 14:7).

> Get wisdom, get understanding; do not forget my words or swerve from them. Do not forsake wisdom, and she will protect you; love her, and she will watch over you. Wisdom is supreme; therefore get wisdom. Though it cost all you have, get understanding. Esteem her, and she will exalt you; embrace her, and she will honor you. She will set a garland of grace on your head and present you with a crown of splendor (Proverbs 4:5-9).

Intellectual growth is one of the foundations of self-esteem. As we learn and apply knowledge, we have a deep sense of fulfillment. Watch a young child when he first begins to read. You will see a new countenance, a new spark. Intellectual competence creates a feeling of worth and security.

> Next to the knowledge that God created us stands another pillar of our self-esteem—the awareness of our abilities and a sense of inner strength. This pillar speaks directly to our need for confidence, it is the knowledge that God gives unique talents to each of us. No two people are exactly alike. Yet every person who has ever walked the face of this earth has been given gifts by God. . . . We can rest in the complete confidence that whatever God intends that we should do, He has given us the ability to accomplish. We can confidently reach out, trying new ideas and tackling new challenges.[1]

If using our minds leads to feelings of confidence, then it is obvious that not using our minds leads to feelings of stagnation or lethargy. People were made to be challenged and when that is not happening, our whole person is affected.

Take Jan's case. Jan was a bright high school student and entered college with a sense of excitement. She loved to study and could often be overheard saying, "Wow! That's interesting." She liked Bible studies and other groups where there was a free flow of ideas. You might say thinking was her bag.

Jan married shortly after college, but that didn't hinder her from launching a stimulating career in interior design. She really felt like she was at the cutting edge. Although she and her husband, Tom, had not planned it that way, Jan became pregnant during the second year of their marriage. She didn't know what to feel. She had always wanted to be a mother, but not right at the time when she was enjoying the challenge of her job. She couldn't help wondering about God's timing.

A healthy, happy baby arrived in due time, and Jan was content for a time to stay home and use her creativity as a mother. She and her husband decided if they wanted two children, they should go ahead and have the other one soon. Their plan worked, and soon Jan was the mother of two—a newborn and a two-year-old.

Jan had never anticipated the change the addition of the second child would make. All of a sudden she felt like a slave. She couldn't even find time to read the newspaper, let alone keep up on the latest books in her field. She began to lose some of her zeal. By the time Tom got home at night, she was almost desperate to talk to an adult for a change. "I think I'm losing my vocabulary," she said.

Things seemed to only get worse, not better. It helped when Timmy got out of diapers, but by the time he was out of diapers, he was into everything else. It wasn't long before Jan hit a severe depression. She began to resent the children, and she was angry toward Tom who always appeared challenged by his work. She was shocked to realize that she had even considered suicide. That just wasn't like her.

Tom began to realize the severity of the situation and sought guidance. I encouraged him to motivate Jan back into the world of ideas. It was a hard decision. He had to change his work schedule some so that he could watch the children while Jan took a refresher class. They also left the children with a sitter one night a week so that they could go out and talk together. He said, "I guess I had forgotten how bright and fun she could be."

Because of Tom's caring for Jan's intellectual needs, they made it. Not without a struggle. But Jan did learn that she could expand her mind even while mothering. Later she returned to work on a part-time basis. She was able to confidently keep her intellect growing because she determined to do so once Tom got her started on the right track.

Intellectual needs are expressed in different ways by different people. Some men become bored in their jobs because of the routine and the lack of intellectual challenge. They often feel they cannot change their jobs because of the economic impact upon the family. This is a real predicament. For some, it contributes to what Conway terms the "Mid-Life Crisis."

> The man approaching mid-life has some strange and difficult times ahead of him. He may negotiate the walk along the unfamiliar top of the brick wall with little trouble, but many men in mid-life feel more like Humpty Dumpty.
> The mid-life crisis is a time of high risk for marriages. It's a time of possible career disruption and extramarital affairs. There is depression, anger, frustration, and rebellion. The crisis is a pervasive thing that seems to affect not only the physical but also the social, cultural, spiritual, and occupational expressions of a man's life.[2]

If you or a friend or family member suffers because of unmet or unchallenged intellectual needs, there are some things you can do. Reading is obviously one of the greatest and cheapest resources. Join study groups. Sit and talk about ideas. Don't get lulled into the same old TV shows with the same old "non-plots." Find friends who challenge your thinking and who see you as interesting.

GIGO is an acronym used in the world of computers. It means "garbage in, garbage out." The same is true of our brains. If you take seriously your need to grow and learn, you can challenge the boredom and the lethargy. You need to be sensitive to the intellectual needs of those close to you, too. Philosopher and writer Os Guinness sums it up nicely.

> Man is a meaning-monger. He is driven by a deep desire for meaning. He can live meaningfully only if he can make sense of his situation at some level. Part of being human is the need to find a framework through which life can be interpreted, so that the bare facts and raw experiences of life are given coherence and meaning.[3]

Emotional—Need to Feel or Experience

Of all the characteristics of human beings, the emotions are the ones most feared and least understood. Literally hundreds of times I have heard people say, "I just wish I didn't feel things."

We know that we have needs in the emotional area, and yet we don't understand our emotions well enough to determine what those needs are. Where should we begin? We need to first accept emotions for what they really are. Swihart gives us a good perspective.

> He could have created us without any capacity for feelings. But then, in a very real sense, we would also have been left without the capacity for relationships, with Him or with each other. Those who seem to lack feelings—guilt, anxiety, love—we often refer to as "inhuman." They seem more like machines or hollow shells than people. It is clear then: We should take delight in our emotional nature. To eliminate emotions would not only rid us of fear of the dark, sadness over death, and anger at inconvenience, but also of satisfaction over a job well done, deep love of one close to us, and hearty laughter at a well told joke. Without emotions, we are hollow men.[4]

I find it helpful to view emotions as vital signs for our lives. They are like temperature or pulse or respiratory rate. They tell us when things are going well, and they tell us when we are in trouble. This concept is expanded in my book, *The Undivided Self.*

Because emotions are so volatile, we often tend to ignore them, hoping that they will go away or somehow care for themselves. This is a mistake. What is needed is not for them to be corrected or for them to go away; what is needed is for them to be understood.

Tournier has pointed out that people often withdraw from each other because they fear being condemned or fear being advised. I believe that this is particularly true when it comes to the emotional area. I don't always understand my emotions in the first place. And I am unwilling to show them to you if I think you will tell me that they don't make sense.

If you want to care for someone's needs in the emotional area, you must hear them out initially. Then you must try to understand the meaning that they place on their emotions. Tournier illustrates how important this can be.

> The husband began by unveiling his anxieties, but, in the face of such ready-made answers, he withdraws. He is crushed in his hope before being able to show his wife all the aspects of a delicate problem. The wife's intention was excellent, but she ruined everything by replying too quickly. She should have listened longer and tried to understand.[5]

The first step then in understanding emotional needs: Listen, and try to understand the feelings from the other person's point of view.

A second step in understanding emotional needs is to take people seriously. The way they feel is the way it is for them, whether the facts support the feelings or not. It also doesn't matter whether you want them to feel that way or not. You can't correct people's feelings. That is a choice they must make.

Recently the real estate office where my wife works was closed. She was upset over the closing and fearful of the process of getting established in a new work environment. She tried to share those feelings with me. I listened for a second or two and said, "Well, you certainly won't have any trouble. You get along so well with people." She looked like she had been kicked in the stomach by a mule.

I knew I had missed the boat, but I didn't know exactly how to care for her and her work loss feeling. Finally she said, "I don't need you to fix it for me. I need you to know I'm scared."

Unfortunately, most men have been trained to try to heal emotions by logically overpowering the other person and helping them see a logical, positive outcome. What is needed is to move alongside and identify with the person's struggle. Sandy said, "I know you know I can make it; and I probably know that, too. That really isn't the point. The point is I'm not sure I can make it without knowing that you care that I'm hurting."

Later my partner Daryl called. He asked Sandy, "What's happening in your life?" She related the story of the office closing, and he responded by saying, "That's going to be hard for you, isn't it?" She felt cared for. She felt understood.

She felt like she could make it. He recognized the fears she had as a serious matter, and she didn't feel condemned.

A third step in understanding emotional needs is questioning without manipulating. A question such as, "You don't really feel that way, do you?" is a manipulating question. It is a back-handed way of telling the person that they *shouldn't* feel a certain way.

Feelings are like a tangled ball of yarn. It would be nice if they were orderly, but you don't straighten them out by grabbing a thread and pulling. You have to gently fluff the ball until you can see the tangles or find the ends. Then untangling is possible.

People's needs for self-understanding are often met when you ask questions about what is going on inside of them. The most caring thing you can possibly say may be, "Talk about it some more." Most people want a hurting person to shut up when he is emotional. They don't want to be made uncomfortable. But if you encourage a person to talk, he will feel accepted and more normal. Ask "what," not "why"! Why questions force people to explain away rather than to understand. Ask them for some specific suggestions as to how you might be helpful. They might not have an answer for you at first, but as they see you are sincere and caring, they may see an area in which you can really help.

The focus of this step is upon increased awareness for you and self-awareness for the hurting person. The issue is *what is*—not *what should be* or *why*.

Once understanding has been broadened, you may realize some specific ways that the person is keeping himself upset. A caring friend is a challenging friend; yet the key is to challenge without conquering.

Questions are much more effective than declarations. Ask the person where he would like to be with his feelings. Ask him to think about how he can get where he wants to be. Ask him how he thinks God can help and how he thinks you can help. Ask him if he can identify some lies that he is telling himself. Teach him to make self-statements which are true.

Remember: Your challenge should leave the person intact. You don't train a kitty with a club. Dead kittens don't learn. Hebrews 10 uses three key words to help us learn how to help each other grow. They are *spur*, *meet*, and *encourage*.

Let us hold unswervingly to the hope we profess, for he
who promised is faithful. And let us consider how we
may spur one another on toward love and good deeds.
Let us not give up meeting together, as some are in the
habit of doing, but let us encourage one another—and
all the more as you see the Day approaching (Hebrews
10:23-25).

To spur someone in the emotional area is to get him to
begin to think of new possibilities, to get him out of his rut.
Meeting together is important because we need one
another's support. And remember; it takes time to meet emotional needs. Listening is time-consuming. To encourage is to
keep the person focused on the possibilities, not just on the
problem. Often your job is to help the person to remember
that God is alive and well and that He will enable the person
to move forward.

The final step is to accept the person in the process of sorting through his feelings. Give him space to be who he is,
where he is, while realizing that he himself doesn't like or
enjoy being upset. Guinness points to the need for loving a
person through difficult periods of life. Although his specific
emphasis is on problems with doubt, the principle applies to
emotional turmoil as well.

Love a person for himself and you can ignore for the moment what his doubt is saying and still take him seriously as a person. When we respond only to the con-
tents of a person's doubt, we are treating him seriously
only insofar as he is a believer or doubter. But when we
respond also to the personal causes of the doubt, we are
taking him seriously as a person.[6]

Bill had been depressed for quite some time. He just didn't
seem to be able to get on top. His friend, Doug, tried to move
close to him, even though he didn't know what to do. At
times Bill seemed to be going from bad to worse, but Doug
stayed close to him and let him have his ups and downs.

After what seemed like an eternity for Doug and for Bill,
Bill began to put things together. His periods of depression
didn't last as long, and he began to take responsibility for his
feelings instead of just letting them control him. Later when
he was asked what was the most helpful thing in his recovery, he said: "Knowing Doug was there and that he cared."

Social—Need to Connect with People

When God observed that it was not good for man to be alone, He gave us a clue as to the nature of man.

> The LORD God said, "It is not good for the man to be alone. I will make a helper suitable for him" (Genesis 2:18).

When God created Eve and thus completed the human team, He acknowledged that man was created to be in relationship with other people. While some people choose to be hermits and other people feel alone even in the city, both of these conditions are contrary to man's basic nature. We were meant to be in contact with others.

I often ask people, "Who are you close to?" Often the reply is, "I have a few friends." If I pursue the issue, I am often surprised to come down to the answer, "I'm really not close to anyone. There are some people around, but I don't really feel like I belong."

It is not hard to recognize this lack of attachment to people when you see an alcoholic asleep against a garbage can in an alley. You can accept that. But what about those times when you see it in yourself or a family member? It is at these times that you begin to understand the need to connect with people more emphatically. It is no longer an academic problem. It is a very personal one.

I found it helpful to look at human contact in three ways: casual, meaningful, and intimate. We have needs in each of these areas.

Casual contact is depicted in figure 1. The two people represented by the circles are only touching at the outer edge. Their inner persons are not affected by the other.

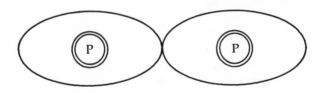

Figure 1—Casual Social Contact

These two people are acquaintances. They are each aware of the other, but they do not really have a meaningful relationship.

A lot has been written about the problem of superficial relationships. Still these are important. Even casual contacts give you a sense of being part of the broader picture. We need to see how others live. It is healthy to get out and mingle even with people you do not know very well. Most relationships start in this way.

Be sensitive to people's needs for casual interaction, even if your needs may fall into one of the categories of deeper involvement. Sometimes it can be very refreshing to be with someone without feeling responsible for that person. You don't have to have either surface or extremely deep contacts. Most people need both.

Relationships become meaningful as the two lives overlap more and more. See figure 2 below.

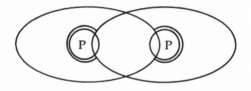

Figure 2—Meaningful Social Contact

This type of relationship usually involves some type of sharing of activities and thoughts. The outer edge of each person overlaps with the other, and there is even an occasional deep interaction as shown by the arrow.

I met a friend in the hallway at church one morning. My question: "How are you today, Vic?"

His answer: "If you really want to take the time I will tell you."

I was somewhat taken back, but I realized that we could have a meaningful relationship if I was willing to invest the time. Our outer lives overlapped, but we were really not invested in each other.

In a meaningful relationship, you look forward to being with that person. This need to "be with" is important. I get together with my advisees at the seminary. I am with a group of parents at our town athletic events. Our small group at church goes to concerts and goes out for pizza together. These are all meaningful relationships. Some of them are handshake relationships. Others are huggy relationships. All have their place.

Meaningful relationships such as these we have described are often called friendships. C. S. Lewis has written about friendship.

> Friendship arises out of mere companionship when two or more of the companions discover that they have in common some insight or interest or even taste which the others do not share and which till that moment, each believed to be his own unique treasure (or burden). The typical expression of opening friendship would be something like, "What? You too? I thought I was the only one."[7]

It is important that such friendships happen inside and outside our families.

As you seek to care for others, be sensitive to their needs for meaningful relationships. Do what you can to facilitate these relationships both with you and with others around you. Don't force them. Just encourage them.

The third type of relationship is an intimate relationship. Intimate relationships involve a sharing of the inner person. When I have an intimate relationship, the other person knows who I am.

We have typically thought of a sexual relationship as the ultimate in intimacy. Such is not the case. In our day and age, many, many people are having sexual relationships. Very few people have intimate relationships. The biblical concept of knowing the other, which often refers to sexual intercourse, had in mind a total exchange of person as symbolized by the sex act in marriage. Sex is intended to symbolize social intimacy.

For our purposes here, we will look at intimacy apart from the symbol of sex. People have a real need for overlap at the inner person as symbolized by figure 3.

Figure 3—Intimate Social Contact

This type of relationship can be found in several different ways. A *good* marriage usually provides this type of interaction. Friendships may become intimate relationships. Relationships within the family are sometimes intimate, such as sibling-sibling or parent-child. The closeness of the relationship can never be determined by the role, only by the interaction. Some of the loneliest, neediest people in the world are married or come from what appear to be good families.

Intimate friends don't talk about the news or the weather. They talk about what is going on with each other. My friend, Dee (Uncle Friesen), calls and asks, "What's going on with you? How are you doing?" I know he cares. We talk about our frustrations. We share our joys. We joke. We philosophize. Sometimes we even cry. This type of relationship is what James and Savary have called third-self friendships.

An intimate relationship such as this sometimes exists between people of the same sex and sometimes between persons of the opposite sex. When the relationship is between persons of the opposite sex and one or both are married, the problem of affection and sexual attraction may become a complicating factor. My wife has several deep friendships with persons of the opposite sex. I am able to encourage her in those friendships because of the intimate and trusting relationship which we have. James and Savary have quoted Henrik Ibsen on this point.

> The costliness of keeping friends does not lie in what one does for them but in what one, out of consideration for them, refrains from doing.[8]

The importance of developing emotionally intimate relationships within marriage cannot be overemphasized. Too many people are married to strangers; they do not interact at the core of their person. Four things are necessary for non-interaction to be corrected. (They will be elaborated in detail in a later chapter.) Greater intimacy requires: (1) taking the risk of knowing and being known; (2) taking the time to be intimate; (3) caring enough to work through the hard times; and (4) valuing the process enough to keep it a priority.

These four things, if practiced, will open up a whole new world of possibilities for having those deep social needs met. Intimacy doesn't happen all at once, but it does happen as the four essentials are maintained.

One final social need is the need to be a part of a group. Figure 4 shows the type of relationship which is needed for personal security and stimulation of personal growth.

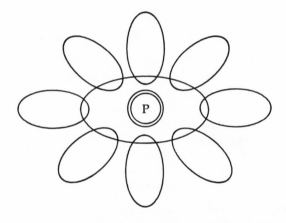

Figure 4—The Need for Group Involvement

The way in which the person relates to various members of the group may differ, but the need for belonging is important. People need to feel included, and they need to feel that they are needed by others. Such group members can test their perceptions of self with a number of people who care but can still provide suggestions regarding the person's behavior.

Sometimes within the marriage relationship, individuals try to have all their social needs met by their mate. This usually does not work, because the mate may not be able to meet all of the needs that his spouse has. Rather than become frustrated by this, the mate would be better off to facilitate the opportunity for his spouse to be involved in a small fellowship group.

I sought for years to help my wife to see her value and spiritual potential. I was frustrated in my effort to encourage; she was frustrated in sensing her worth. It was only after she became involved with a circle of women at church that she was able to grasp God's love and her specialness. She needed the group. When I talked to her, she expected to hear encouraging things. She treated them as compliments any husband would give. When individuals in the group spoke, she listened because she didn't expect them to be positive.

Involvement with a group will not take the place of a close, caring relationship with a spouse or a friend. But it is a needed and helpful supplement.

Spiritual—Need to Connect with God

The Westminster Confession states that the purpose of man is to glorify God and enjoy Him forever. This purpose is stated from God's point of view, but it follows that God's creative purpose for man corresponds with a similar need He created in man. We need to love God and glorify Him! We are not complete apart from our connectedness with God in this manner. In fact, we cannot fully understand and know ourselves until we relate to God in a personal way. A popular theologian urges us to consider this prime relationship.

> "This is true love to any one," said Tillotson, "to do the best for him we can." This is what God does for those He loves—*the best He can*; and the measure of the best that God can do is omnipotence! Thus faith in Christ introduces us into a relation big with incalculable blessing, both now and for eternity.[9]

The awareness of God's personal love is the greatest possession you can have. Because our relationship with God is so personal, we often neglect the other person's relationship with God. We care for people in all the areas of their needs but sometimes neglect their spiritual needs.

People want the encouragement and opportunity to grow in the spiritual area, in spite of how personal it is to them. There is assurance in knowing that others love the same God and are also struggling to learn how to relate to Him more completely. Husbands and wives need to share their faith with each other as do friends. This sharing provides the basis for the deepening of personal friendship.

In seeking to understand the needs of others, it is important to remember that their needs vary from day to day. And needs are highly personalized. You cannot assume that your friend's or spouse's needs are the same as yours.

Look carefully at the physical, emotional, social, intellectual, and spiritual aspects of the life of the other person. You will find many opportunities to care. If you have trouble identifying a person's needs, it is better to ask him than to guess. If it seems awkward to ask about people's needs, it might be helpful to remember this: Even asking about someone is an act of caring.

Chapter 4, Notes

[1]S. Bruce Narramore, *You're Someone Special* (Grand Rapids: Zondervan, 1978), pp. 130-131.

[2]Jim Conway, *Men in Mid-Life Crisis* (Elgin, Ill.: David C. Cook, 1978), p. 17.

[3]Os Guinness, *In Two Minds* (Downers Grove, Ill.: InterVarsity Press, 1976), pp. 141-142.

[4]Phillip J. Swihart, *How to Live with Your Feelings* (Downers Grove, Ill.: InterVarsity Press, 1976), pp. 10-11.

[5]Paul Tournier, *To Understand Each Other*, pp. 22-23.

[6]Guinness, *In Two Minds*, pp. 225, 227.

[7]C. S. Lewis, *Four Loves* (New York: Harcourt, Brace, Jovanovich, Inc., 1960), p. 96.

[8]Muriel James and Louis Savary, *The Heart of Friendship* (New York: Harper and Row, 1978), p. 70.

[9]J. I. Packer, *Knowing God* (Downers Grove, Ill.: InterVarsity Press, 1973), p. 115.

5

Friends Need Caring, Too

**Reaching out is
hard to do**

ONE OF THE GREATEST needs that people have is to learn to better care for their friends. Friendship without caring is like eating turkey without dressing or playing basketball without a hoop. It leaves something to be desired.

> Caring is not the same as using the other person to satisfy one's own needs. Neither is it to be confused with such things as well-wishing, or simply having an interest in what happens to another. Caring is a process of helping others grow and actualize themselves. It is a transforming experience. Care and concern are expected between friends, especially in times of crisis. . . . When things get rough, friends are likely to look at each other for nurturing. When self-esteem is low, they look for encouragement. When emotions are frayed, friends need lifting up.[1]

Because no legal or blood ties link friends together, it is often difficult to know when and how to get involved with friends in a caring way. Knowing how to nurture, encourage, or support is difficult.

In this chapter, we will examine the unique opportunities to care for friends. We will give some specific answers to the how and when questions that snarl our efforts to help friends. We will also look at three types of friendships: male-male, female-female, and male-female. The peculiar characteristics of each type of friendship will be examined.

The Unique Opportunity

During the last decade, a group of people increased in number, influence, and importance in our community. We call them simply—singles. This number has increased because of marriage breakdowns and a rapid divorce rate, but also because many people are choosing to marry later in life or remain single. Churches are beginning to see the opportunity to reach out and meet some of the needs of the millions of people who call themselves single. One of the most obvious ways to care for the single person is to build a strong friendship with him or her.

Caring through friendship, however, is not limited to singles. Husbands, wives, children, grandparents all need caring as well. Our depersonalized society with its lack of trust has created a need for people of all ages and in all walks of life to learn how to care for those around them. Yet we are plagued with fear that prevents us from taking a good look at the needs of those with whom we brush shoulders every day. On the morning news the other day, I heard of another suicide. A 14-year-old boy shot himself at his high school. The only explanation he gave before his death was "no one loves me."

When Jesus spoke of loving one another, He gave a command, not a suggestion.

> A new commandment I give you: love one another. As I have loved you, so you must love one another (John 13:34).

If there is anything that is obvious about our modern society, it is that there is more talk about love than there is action. Love is a filler word. It has no meaning because it has no substance. The apostle John wrote specifically to this point.

> This is how we know what love is: Jesus Christ laid down his life for us. And we ought to lay down our lives for our brothers. If anyone has material possessions and sees his brother in need but has no pity on him, how can the love of God be in him? Dear children, let us not love with words or tongue but with actions and in truth (1 John 3:16-18).

Caring is love in action plus kind words. If you think both aren't needed, visit an elementary school. The words and the actions are not compassionate and caring. They are cruel. Children who grow up under these kinds of circumstances without a balancing amount of love from friends or family will be lonely and self-critical. They themselves will not know how to care for their friends.

Try an experiment in friendship. Befriend a neighbor child or adolescent. Be kind to him. Show interest in him. Talk with him. You will be amazed at how quickly you will have a new friend.

I made the effort to show some interest in a youngster from our community. He entered a wrestling tournament which his dad could not attend. I had never met him before, but I went to the matches. Quickly I became his father figure. Two years later, at the same tournament, he was not alone. He was a leader of several younger boys. I was amazed, however, at the way he reached out to be friendly to me. With warm feelings I realized that this fourteen-year-old strong man really cared for me. I had invested so little, and I received so much back in return. God returns care for care.

In a day in which people will not even step out of an apartment to aid those in trouble, your love and caring can make a great deal of difference to others. And to you. Yours is a unique opportunity to connect your life to friends and potential friends who as yet are strangers. The key is to take the first steps.

My daughter Marcie began to tutor handicapped teenagers while she was a senior in high school. She grew excited about the opportunity to help others reach their potential. As her parents, we realized that the youngsters with whom she was working were also having a profound effect on Marcie. Her caring was providing her with a unique opportunity to be cared for by others.

If you take the risk to care you will usually receive as much as you give. Many lonely, depressed people find relief only as they begin to get outside of themselves and to minister to others by caring. It is a unique, untapped opportunity.

Often we think of caring only in times of emergencies. My memory as a child will not let me forget how our neighbors came to our aid when our farm home burned. They moved alongside; they met our physical and many of our emotional needs. As I have grown up, however, I have wondered: Was that as caring as the acts of kindness that were shown when the need was not as dramatic and painful? I remember neighbors sharing cakes and short visits spontaneously. Those times helped my parents know how much they belonged to that community. Societal changes have robbed us of many of the joys of caring. Now the state does for people what friends and neighbors used to do. The opportunities are still there, however. We need only to look for them. Friendship is still a live option.

> Yet, friends still show many examples of caring for each other. For example, friends still help each other move. They bring food to a sick friend, and drive a friend's children in a car pool. They volunteer to help friends in a project, or babysit for their children.[2]

Learning How to Care for a Friend

Caring is a set of skills to be learned and practiced. Many people make the mistake of thinking it is something that you are born with, and that you naturally care for friends. That's not true.

Let's start by learning to perceive others' needs. There is nothing quite as obvious, and yet as hidden, as the needs of a friend. To discover them, you must listen. Listen—not just with your ears, but with your eyes and the rest of your senses as well. Use your mind. Think about your friend. Try to put yourself into his position in life. Last—use your mouth. Don't be afraid to ask. There are no other words which carry encouragement as do the words, "What may I do to help?" or "How can I be supportive of you right now?"

You may also need to encourage your friend to express his needs more openly. You cannot read his mind. You need to let him know that you will not be able to meet all his needs, but you would like the opportunity to meet the ones you can.

Cedric was very nervous one morning. He was pacing back and forth from one office to another. My first thought was, "What is wrong with him?" I didn't do anything to reach out because I hadn't perceived his need.

Finally, I realized Cedric had a need and said, "I've got time to talk if you do." He seemed relieved already as we grabbed our coffee cups and began to talk. He was nervous because he needed a sounding board. I was delighted to listen. But first I had to see his need.

Caring is not a haphazard operation. This second characteristic is important. It takes planning. Decisions have to be made about how to express caring, and plans for action need to be thought through. When I was courting my wife, I was quite skilled at perceiving her needs and deciding how I would like to meet those needs. In fact, it was my favorite subject at school. I studied hard and it was a joyful experience. This same type of observing and planning is necessary in caring friendships.

Recently when my son had surgery, a friend, Eunice, delivered a package to the hospital. Or I should say had the package delivered by one of her friends. She was out of town on the day of the surgery, but her caring came through because she had taken time to plan. The cards and the friendship gifts were delivered right on time, even though she was three thousand miles away. Did we feel special? You know we did! Sometimes I miss caring opportunities because I don't start by planning. I live with regrets and missed opportunities.

A third aspect of learning to care is overcoming the emotional obstacles which block caring behaviors. There are times when I don't feel like caring. I let inertia set in. At other times I may be hurt or angry or feel that my friend should be doing more to care for me. It is easy to rationalize not caring right now because you don't feel like it at this moment.

Caring, like most forms of learning, has both a behavioral and an emotional component. We must learn what to do (the behavior), and we must learn how to manage our emotions so as to carry out the caring behavior. Sometimes hurt or anger are the enemies. Sometimes the problem is fear of failure. Regardless of the hindering emotion, we must still learn to deal with it if we are to learn to care.

The fourth step of caring is the proof of the pudding. It is carrying out the caring action. Yes, actions do speak louder than words. Caring actions speak louder than good intentions. I do not believe it is taking liberty with Scripture to say "caring" without deeds is dead (see James 2:26b). Allow God to get you excited about caring for your friends. Get outside yourself and begin to do for others. Don't care for someone because you feel you have to—but because you get to.

We have a close friend who likes pigs. He used to raise them when he was younger. As Sandy and I walked through a store one day, we saw a belt buckle with a pig on it. We looked at each other almost simultaneously, knowing that we wanted to buy the buckle because it would tell our friend we feel he is special. We remember his interests and take seriously his likes and dislikes.

What else can I say? If you see a friend with a need and know how to care for it, do it. The more you care the more you learn to care. Your caring will not always be acknowledged or appreciated by your friend. But don't let that stop you from seeking to become the kind of caring person you long to be.

The next step is to review the results of your caring efforts and solidify the gains. You will find mixed results. Some of the things you did may have been very successful. Other efforts may seem to have been in vain. You will misperceive needs and make plans that don't pan out. Don't be discouraged. Concentrate on what you did that was successful or consistent with who you want to be. Thank God for the progress you are making in becoming a caring person. Let Paul's words to the Galatians guide you in your effort.

> Let us not become weary in doing good, for at the proper time we will reap a harvest if we do not give up. Therefore, as we have opportunity, let us do good to all people, especially to those who belong to the family of believers (Galatians 6:9-10).

Learning When to Care

The question of when to care for a friend seems silly on the surface. Any time is the time for caring. Yet we often hesitate, not knowing when to reach out to others. Because caring is such a personal matter, we fear being rejected. We look for the opportune moment which may never come.

When should you seek to show caring?

When you feel like it?
When you don't feel like it?
When you see an opportunity?
When you see a need?
When you want to strengthen a relationship?

When you feel the leading of the Holy Spirit?
In good times?
In bad times?
When it is convenient?
When it is inconvenient?

The answer to each question is yes. You can care during all of these times. In fact, if you seek to care in various circumstances and difficult times, caring may become a way of life. Caring in this manner may change your life. It may become the positive addition you need to find new meaning and purpose. Remember, Jesus said, "I tell you the truth, whatever you did for one of the least of these brothers of mine, you did for me" (Matthew 25:40).

If you seek to care and your timing seems to be off, don't become discouraged. The problem may be your friend's, not yours. Even within marriages, we often misread the other person's needs at a given moment. Back off long enough for the person to be ready to receive what you have to give. Comments like the following may be helpful to you.

"I think I picked a bad time." "Would you like me to call you back tomorrow?" Or "Would you like to call me when you are ready?"

Give people options. But clearly communicate your desire to stay close to them or to minister to their needs. Staying close to a person when they are not sure they want you there may be risky for you. It is also a strong source of support for the person in need.

Caring for Males

I often hear women say, "I just don't know how to care for men. They always try to be so self-sufficient. They won't let you get close."

In a lot of ways, this is true. Our culture teaches men to appear strong even when they do not feel strong. We often repress our needs so deeply that we cannot admit them to ourselves.

> Males learn that caring is considered to be a female responsibility. As a result they may overreact against either giving or receiving care. This learning tends to be reinforced even in many very caring homes during pre-

adolescence, when kissing, hugging, and holding are withheld from boys. The peer group becomes a powerful influence during this stage, and even boys whose parents continue to be affectionate may imitate other boys and reject affection. However these messages are delivered, few boys escape learning that caring is the province of females and that they should seldom yield to the need to receive or give care.[3]

Men often withdraw when they feel needy while women sometimes seek closeness. Men often try to work out their frustrations through physical activity or other forms of escapism such as drinking or video games. The unfortunate thing about these substitute activities is that they don't really work. They still leave the itches unscratched.

If you have a male friend, learn to spend time with him when he is trying to withdraw. Be available and yet don't force him to talk until he is ready. When he does talk don't try to fix things for him. Just be there. Possibly ask some questions or make some comments that will show you know he is struggling.

I have found it most helpful when my friends approach me to declare their availability and then leave the next move to me. My friend Cedric often says, "You look troubled today! Are you okay?" If I say, "I'm okay," he doesn't say, "Now wait a minute. You really look sick!" He accepts my answer for the moment even though he may know better.

Because I know Cedric cares and is approachable, I have often gone back to him a short while after he has stated his concern for me. I usually say something like, "I wasn't being straight with you a while ago. I'm worried about my son," or "I'm having trouble with my class this term. It just isn't flowing." Cedric isn't afraid to get close—to touch me emotionally or physically with a big bear hug. He also isn't afraid to give me space.

Dr. Charles Swindoll tells of a time when he was very depressed and unwilling to relate to anyone. A friend came to him and said, "We are going for a drive. You don't have to talk unless you want to, but you are going with me." They spent several hours in silence. This time was vital, however, to Dr. Swindoll's being able to finally open up to himself, his God, and his friend.

Humor can also be vital in caring for your male friends.

Sometimes men accept what is presented through humor when they cannot deal with issues head on.

My friend Becky is always there with a joke. Sometimes they are just for fun—something she and I can share together. Other times her jokes may have a more specific purpose—either to tell me something or to help me realize that I am taking life too seriously. I don't feel smothered, and yet I know she is there.

Males often withdraw from caring relationships if they feel things are being overdone. Men usually have been spoiled by their mothers, and they resist being mothered by their friends.

> If one of us gives a good bit more caring than the other needs, that tends to feel like smothering: Oh, you poor thing. I just feel so bad for you; I'm sure you're not quite strong enough to do it. I know I just took your temperature, but we can't be too careful, now can we? Or: A heavy dose of hugging when the need is slight.[4]

If you make a mistake in caring such as smothering, don't let that stop your caring. Admit the mistake openly to the person whether male or female. Agree to try to find the most helpful level of involvement. For example, "I really pushed you to talk yesterday and, looking back on it, I am quite sure it wasn't very helpful. I'm willing to back off. Can you tell me some things I might have done that would have been more productive for you or for us?"

Are there unique ways to care for males? Probably not ways which are unique. There are certain important emphases.

1. Remember that men will often resist admitting their needs. That doesn't mean they don't have them. Stay close until these needs can be brought to the surface.

2. Remember that involvement through activities may be the open door for males.

3. Remember to be frank and honest without being patronizing. Don't be afraid to call your male friend to honesty.

4. Remember to be available. Your male friend may not pursue you, so you need to find some ways to communicate with him.

5. Remember to be positive. Show him the better way. Most men resist being with friends of either sex if their

friends are corrective or negative. Optimism is a great healer and a great communicator of caring.

6. Remember to communicate to your male friend how he can care for you. Many men want to be caring, but they haven't learned how. Providing some suggestions will be appreciated if done in the right way.

Daryl sometimes says to me, "Can we talk tomorrow? I want you to think through a decision with me." I feel valued by his confidence in me and he feels valued by my willingness to listen. This mutuality of respect is what it is all about.

Caring for Females

It is said that females are very intuitive and feelings-oriented. This type of generalization is probably not harmful if it is not applied too strictly. My wife is emotional and intuitive, but she also has a great mind. She likes to work with ideas, and she likes to be taken seriously as a thinker.

Caring for females often involves affirming them in seeing themselves as total people. There is a strong need to get away from stereotypes and deal with a woman as she really is. If she does not know who she really is, there is a need to allow her to find herself through the friendship. Don't force her to be a certain way. As a male, I am aware of many ways women are told, subtly or not so subtly, that they are to be a certain way. I reject this.

My wife is a strong, confrontive woman. What a crime for her to be anything less. She is also the most caring person I know. What a crime for her not to be able to express that aspect of her person. Caring for her is to provide an atmosphere in which she can be who she is—strong and caring—and then see how her caring and her confrontation best blend. This is a great adventure for both of us.

Because women are often trained by their environment to express their feelings, they need friendships in which they are listened to and heard. Unfortunately, many of our female friends believe their feelings are not always taken seriously by their friends—especially males.

Whether their feelings are objective or not is what some of your female friends may be experiencing. An active caring plan for them must take that into account.

Although guidelines for caring for females may not be totally distinctive from those for males, here are some items for careful consideration.

1. Listen to hear where the woman is. This is not for the purpose of telling her where she should be, but to enjoy who she is.

2. Once you have discovered where your female friend is coming from, take her seriously. Ask her where she would like to be with her feelings.

3. When you have helped her to articulate where she would like to be, then challenge her to take the necessary steps to get there.

4. Challenge her to use all of her person: mind, emotions, choices, and behavior.

5. Don't fall into the trap of correcting or loving conditionally. This is especially deadly for the male who wants to care for the female. You may destroy that which you admire the most.

Caring in Male-Female Relationships

One of the most difficult tasks we face in our sexually-oriented society is to learn to care for members of the opposite sex. We tend to withdraw because of fear of involvement. Or we get involved, but only in exploitive ways.

I believe very strongly that every person needs opposite sex friends. When I say every person, I am including those who are married. My wife has numerous friendships with males which are wholesome and growth-producing for her, for me, and for her male friends.

One of the difficulties in establishing and maintaining such friendships is that we, as a society, tend to label any heterosexual interactions. What God intended as natural is now quite unnatural. I believe that the close, nonsexual interaction which Jesus had with Mary Magdalene and other women should serve as a model for caring in male-female relationships. You may recall from the Gospel of John (chapter 4) that Jesus was not afraid to approach the Samaritan woman at the well. This flew in the face of the prevailing social customs both in terms of ethics and male-female contact. His proper manner, in the midst of criticism, should guide us.

C. S. Lewis adeptly points out that friendships between people of the opposite sex may develop into erotic love. Fear of this happening, however, may prevent persons of different sexes from experiencing the joy of seeing the same truth. He pictures these relationships: "Hence we picture lovers face to face but friends side by side; their eyes look ahead."[5]

I believe people need the experience of being side by side with persons of both the same sex and the opposite sex before they are ready to look face to face into a romantic relationship. Both types of relationships are important. Romance which grows without friendship may be planted in very shallow soil.

My counseling with persons who have never been married has helped me to come to this understanding: Many people do not marry because they are afraid of being rejected if they are themselves. Friendship creates an atmosphere of love where one learns that it is okay to be the unique person that God has made you to be.

I also believe it is important to interact with persons of the opposite sex of all ages. Through these interactions at differing age levels, you come to know yourself better.

One more thing. We need to accept relationships with friends where they are; don't push friendships to deeper levels than they should be too quickly. In this regard it is important not to put pressure on opposite sex friends by inferring that they may become romantic. People need to learn about relating to others first. Adding pressure and forcing someone to burn a lot of emotional energy about romantic aspects of a relationship is unfair and unwise.

People are at different points in their friendships with the opposite sex. I have stated that Sandy and I are comfortable about developing opposite sex friendships. We have, however, gone through the agony of one or more of those friendships being clouded by romance. Had we lacked a deep love for each other and a open communication style in our marriage, this could have been very harmful. Here is a general rule: Relationships with which both of you are not comfortable should be avoided. But don't steer away from opposite sex relationships. Supporting each other in relationships which have productive potential—whether they are the same or opposite sex—is healthy and desirable.

A second word of caution comes here. Be sure that you and your opposite sex friend have the same agenda, the same idea about the relationship. There are some people who "collect friends" but are really looking for romance. There are others who try to build their ego by "collecting people." They aren't prepared to look for an honest, growth-producing interaction.

> That is why those pathetic people who simply "want friends" can never make any. The very condition of having friends is that we should want something else besides friends. Where the truthful answer to the question *Do you see the same truth?* would be "I see nothing and I don't care about the truth; I only want a friend," no friendship can arise—though affection, of course, may. There would be nothing for the friendship to be *about;* and the friendship must be about something, even if it were only an enthusiasm for dominoes or white mice. Those who have nothing can share nothing; those who are going nowhere can have no fellow-travelers.[6]

In summary, I believe male-female relationships which focus on friendships and caring are invaluable to our growth as persons. They help us find our meaning along the broader spectrum of human experience. When they become exploitive, they have ceased to be valid friendships. Caution, not fear, should accompany our care for the opposite sex. Should we refuse to trust God here, we will miss an important area of relationships.

Managing Your Time

You have been taking this book seriously. You have been considering new possibilities for caring relationships. And now you have probably reached a point of utter frustration.

How can you possibly act on all that you are reading? How can you possibly care for all the people around you, who need your care?

The answer is simple. You can't. You must set caring priorities just as you have set priorities for other areas of your life. Rather than feel guilty about all the opportunities you have overlooked or will overlook, decide what you would like to do in the area of caring for friends. Then try to limit your relationships to a feasible number.

I believe each person needs one or two indepth caring relationships. That doesn't mean you cannot be caring to those with whom your relationship is more superficial. It just means that the sharing of your caring time must be monitored, and some relationships can't be of the deep, caring types. Limit yourself to what you can accomplish.

It is also important to maintain relationships which meet your needs. You cannot produce water from a dry well. Some people just naturally prime your pump. Make sure you include these people in your relationship patterns. They will give you energy to be more caring to others.

If you wish to care for a broad spectrum of friends, you will need to strike a delicate balance between giving and receiving. Both your casual and your deep relationships must be balanced as well.

Encourage a friend with whom you can talk to help you reach out more effectively. Whether you are married or single, your friends need caring, too. Your challenge: Develop a lifestyle of sensitivity which gives you the freedom to be a friend—who cares.

Chapter 5, Notes

[1]Muriel James and Louis Savary, *The Heart of Friendship* (New York: Harper and Row, 1978), pp. 78-79.

[2]Ibid, p. 79.

[3]Richard C. Nelson, *Choosing: A Better Way to Live* (Lake Park, Fl.: Guidelines Press, 1977), p. 94.

[4]Ibid, p. 91.

[5]C. S. Lewis, *Four Loves* (New York: Harcourt, Brace, Jovanovich, Inc., 1960), p. 98, n. 1.

[6]Ibid, p. 98, n. 2.

6

Eliminating Nonproductive Approaches

_____

**What feels good for you
may not be caring for them**

WHEN I WAS a teenager, I spent lots of hours in our car
with my father. He was my on-the-site driver's ed instructor.
In training me for the road, he stressed several points of the
driving art as he knew it. One was the importance of timing. I
had a tendency to put on the brake when I should have been
depressing the clutch. At other times, I would find my foot on
the accelerator when I should have been braking. All the
functions of driving needed the timing element to prevent a
horrible driver from being loosed on the community.

My father emphasized another principle in driving: Eliminate nonproductive approaches for getting out of a tight
place. When I first tried driving on snow and ice, I would use
too much gas and end up getting stuck. Then my father
would slide over and take the wheel, using an altogether different approach. He would simply let the car idle its way out
of the frozen ruts. My approach was nonproductive. He re-
placed it with his more productive way.

Sandy and I have observed a similar phenomenon in the
caring process. Many people's attempts to care meet with
little or no success. Their efforts may be like my giving our car
the gas. It was not always the best solution.

There are some behaviors you see as caring because you
would like to be cared for in that way. But they may be totally
nonproductive with your spouse or friend.

When Sandy and I were first married, she used to scratch my back. Now she enjoyed a good back scratch. But she did not realize that for me it was more of an irritation than a pleasure. When I finally got up enough courage to tell her, she was relieved. She certainly hadn't been enjoying my lack of response.

There are other times when we try to imitate the ways we see others care. This, too, may be nonproductive. The needs of your friend or spouse may be totally different than the needs of others you've seen cared for. Caring is a very individualized process; what worked for one person may not be helpful in the new situation.

Most women love to receive phone calls from their husbands. One friend of ours, however, was very upset that her husband called her so often. "He always calls just when I get the children down," she said. "Doesn't he realize that is the only time I get a chance to rest?" The husband had to learn to time his caring more carefully. Hearing from him was important, but needing to rest was important, too. After talking it over, they found a time for a telephone contact that both could agree to. She didn't feel irritated, and he didn't feel rejected.

In the following pages we will discuss several different ways that people try to show caring. Each activity is normally nonproductive, regardless of the intentions behind it. For each ineffective caring approach we will present one or two alternatives. The serious reader may wish to try these in place of the nonproductive approach.

Correctiveness

A husband or wife often corrects his mate publicly and then implies that it was only for his mate's good. "I didn't want you to embarrass yourself," one wife stated.

Sandy is a great storyteller, but she has been known to forget pertinent details. Especially if it interrupts the story line. I used to feel my duty as a husband was to be the guardian of the facts. This often resulted in my correcting her stories publicly. I often hurt her, though I wanted to help her.

Let me show you some scenarios. If Sandy said she had canned five bushels of pickles, I would help her by reminding her that I only counted three. If she said the house was 50 feet high, I would remind her that it measured only 28 feet, 6 inches. Instead of feeling helped, she felt unloved and disrespected. We talked about it on many occasions, and I began to realize the importance of enjoying her stories and letting her be herself. When I changed, she became more open to me. To my amazement she began to ask for pertinent facts when she could do so without ruining her story.

Correctiveness is rarely a loving behavior. It usually tears down the person even when we have intended it for good. It is especially damaging when it is carried out publicly or in front of other family members. If you find yourself caring only by correcting, take a look at the reasons behind your behavior. You may be competing with your spouse or friend. This results in trying to keep the other person in line rather than in trying to build him or her up. Regardless of the reason, look for a better option.

What are some caring options to correctiveness?

Sandy and I have discovered several new possibilities. First, support and encourage rather than correct and castigate. When I began to appreciate Sandy's great ability as a storyteller, I didn't need to correct her. From my point of view, who cares whether she canned three or five bushels of pickles? She is a vivacious, alive person who can make even a story of canning pickles an event we all have to hear about. As I have encouraged her to be herself, she has become more careful about facts without losing her zest for life.

Both of us now feel an openness to one another in this area. Sandy wrote a Christmas letter stating I had just finished roofing our house, our 100-foot high house. I saw the card before it went to the printer, and I could not help asking her about her description. "Honey," I asked, "How tall is our house?"

"It must be at least 100 feet," she said. When I told her it was only 35 to 40 feet high, she said, "Well, who would be impressed with that?" We had a good laugh, and both of us knew we had found an open way to communicate that was not harshly critical.

A second alternative to correctiveness is asking questions. When I asked Sandy how tall the house was, she didn't feel put down. She just realized that she hadn't thought it through very well. Then I dropped the subject, and let her deal with the new information.

Correctiveness is a great relationship killer. Monitor yourself carefully. Being an encourager may rejuvenate your marriage or your friendship.

Eliminating correctiveness does not mean that there will not be any confrontation. You cannot have a caring relationship without effective confrontation. It does mean, however, that the confrontation will not take the form of ruling over the other person.

> Caring differs from ruling in that the intent is to help more than to lead. If I make a caring choice with you, you should feel that the intent was clearly helpful. "Don't forget your briefcase," is an example of a choice I might make in which caring and ruling overlap. I may see it as caring, while you may see it as ruling. The two choices may also merge when I make a suggestion, when I prevent you from doing what you wish, and when I try to guard you.[1]

When you find a need to correct or to rule, it is helpful to ask yourself what purpose the correction has for you. Sometimes we tell ourselves that we are correcting for the sake of the other person. In reality, we could be correcting because it makes us feel better.

Rescue

Another nonproductive approach to caring is what I call rescue or "fix it." Sometimes when Sandy tries to share her feelings with me, I get overinvolved. I feel I must do something for her. I assume that she is letting me know she wants something done. In reality, however, she may just want me to know she hurts.

I often share with Sandy or a friend some of my work frustrations. I do so not to get help. I just need them to say they are with me or that they will pray for me. Sometimes I may need advice. But I should ask for it. And my friend or spouse should ask if I want it.

Rescue or "fix it" communicates to the person, "You do not respect me or my ability to control my life." A better response is to leave the person feeling confident in his ability to handle the feelings or do what is necessary to take care of the situation. The key is to avoid being underinvolved (retreat) or overinvolved (giving unwanted advice). Neither of these approaches is productive.

One important alternative to playing "fix it" is asking the person what his needs are. This will be awkward at first, but is a very important skill to learn.

When I first began to ask Sandy what her needs were after she shared a particular hurt, she was somewhat annoyed and slightly angry. As time went on, though, she could see that my question forced her to think through her needs more carefully. We now share our needs along with our expectations more freely; and both of us feel less inclined to play Mr. "fix it."

A second alternative to rescue or "fix it" is to ask the person what he hopes will happen. If your spouse or friend is really looking for you to fix it, he will tell you at this point. Or he may be able to think through what is really needed at this point.

Recently I asked Sandy what she would like to see happen in our marriage. She said, "I'd like to see you show some responsibility." Ouch! I fought off the temptation to shout at her and asked her where I could show more responsibility. Expecting a "fix it" answer, I was stunned by her response.

What Sandy wanted and what I had thought about doing were miles apart. I thought she wanted me to work around the house more. But she equated responsibility with spending more time with the children. Diving into work would have further avoided this responsibility as it moved me more out of the children's reach. Imagine the hurt and frustration we could have inflicted on each other if this had happened.

There may be times when I need to fix it for my friend or my wife. Usually I just need to stick by them.

Indulgence

Indulging a person is not caring for him. Indulgence is letting a person be nonproductive and less than he could be.

Indulgence is the opposite of tough love. During the course of life, people have to do hard things: things like being honest, coping with depression, or learning to walk again following an accident. Fear and anxiety will show up unwanted, but expected. A person feels he can't make it. He may even wish he was dead. As Christians, we often long for heaven only when the going gets tough.

If someone you love is having difficulty, you may indulge them or even rescue them. The question is, is this the caring thing to do? I think not! When you prevent someone from facing a hard situation, you cause him to be weaker, not stronger. Calling him to courage and supporting his courageous acts is the caring thing to do.

God does not indulge us by taking us out of our difficulties. Rather He stays with us as we face our difficulties. Indulgence would produce dependency out of weakness while His firm support in the pressure produces trust and strength. Notice what Paul the apostle had to say about God's unwillingness to indulge him.

> To keep me from becoming conceited because of these surpassingly great revelations, there was given me a thorn in my flesh, a messenger of Satan, to torment me. Three times I pleaded with the Lord to take it away from me. But he said to me, "My grace is sufficient for you, for my power is made perfect in weakness." Therefore I will boast all the more gladly about my weaknesses, so that Christ's power may rest on me (2 Corinthians 12:7-9).

Even in the face of shortage, Paul was able to stay in there with God's support.

> I know what it is to be in need, and I know what it is to have plenty. I have learned the secret of being content in any and every situation, whether well fed or hungry, whether living in plenty or in want. I can do everything through him who gives me strength (Philippians 4:12-13).

Indulgence as a caring strategy teaches people to be the kind of person they hate. Eventually, they are the kind of person you hate.

One man said, "I just hate it when I am weak."

I asked, "Why don't you become stronger?"

His response was quite simple. "I don't have to! I know my wife will pick up all the pieces. She always has."

Caring says you can make it. You can be who you would really like to be. I will pray for you, support you, and help you see progress. I will give you lemonade as you run the race, not as you sit in the gutter wishing you were running. Caring reinforces people for effort, not for inertia.

What then are some alternatives to indulgence?

First, be an optimistic encourager. Help people state what they would like to be. Then cheer them along the way to the goal.

When one of our sons was young he said, "Dad, being good is hard."

"That's true, son," I said. "But just because it is hard doesn't mean that we are going to let you be bad. We will help you learn to be good."

Suppose a friend has a problem with irrational outbursts of anger. She doesn't need indulgence; she doesn't like herself when she acts that way. What she needs is encouragement to respond differently and to know that she is making progress.

Second, help the person set some goals. Some people can be encouraged—they know what they would like to be and how they would like to act. Other people need to see the options in front of them before you can encourage them.

When people ask me for support, I question them as to their goals and how I can help them reach what they want. If they don't know, they may be looking for indulgence and not support. You can support a person when they are trying to walk. You cannot support a person who is trying to lie in a heap. You can only carry them.

Carrying a person may be a caring response for a brief period of time. It is no substitute for helping the person develop his own goals and the desire to make it. The goal-setting process encourages strength and increases self-esteem; indulgence is detrimental to both.

Smothering

Smothering or pampering is another common nonproductive approach. To smother is to block off air. Without air, it is impossible to grow. Preventing growth is obviously not caring for the person.

There are two common forms of smothering which come thinly disguised as caring: (1) taking responsibility away from the person, and (2) controlling the person by the things you do for them.

When a person is an infant, it is natural to smother him

with attention, do things for him, and take full responsibility. We cuddle him and coddle him. This is good. In fact, research has shown that without cuddling, infants will not reach their full physical potential.

This type of relationship becomes detrimental, however, when we continue to treat children, adolescents, or adults like infants. Smothering often feels good for the one trying to care. If we enjoy it, we may continue in this way without taking a close look at the consequences.

What about taking responsibility away from the person?

Jan and Jim have been married for twelve years. The early years were very happy. Their differences were apparent but didn't really cause them many problems. Jan was a worrier at times, while her husband showed signs of being a dreamer. Neither took this difference very seriously because they stayed on top of their relationship.

With the arrival of a child, Jan became even more conservative. Unfortunately, the happiness of sharing the new life masked that difference. Jan didn't mind Jim working long hours at the job because she knew he was happy serving people.

Eventually the job situation changed. What had been a relaxed and content relationship tensed as the economic pressures began to mount. Jim found a new job fairly soon, but it just wasn't like the old one. He really wasn't very happy in the pressures of the new situation. He began to make noises about quitting that job, and he began dropping hints that Jan could do more than just stay home. After all! What was there to do around the house now that the baby was in preschool?

Jan began to change from being tense to being afraid. At the same time, Jim's dreaming increased as a means of counteracting his displeasure with the job situation. Conflicts exploded more frequently and more openly. The nature of Jan and Jim's relationship subtly began to change from a husband-wife companionship to a parent-child control situation.

Jan began to take too much responsibility for Jim. Her fears motivated her to begin trying to control his dreams, though the dreams helped him persist with his job. He, in turn, became more disoriented and at times acted more and more like a child. He felt her lack of respect and resented the control.

The tension mounted. Jan spent hours preparing logical arguments as to why they shouldn't follow Jim's dreams. The more hard-nosed and logical she became, the more he resented it. They developed the uneasy ache that said they really weren't enjoying each other any more. Although he didn't recognize it, Jim became less responsible because he really didn't have to be responsible. His "mother" was taking care that no mistakes were made. She thought that she was caring for Jim and for herself; in reality it was hurting them both, holding them back as a couple.

I directed her to question herself. She needed to examine the type of relationship she wanted with Jim and the effects of her behavior on that relationship.

I asked, "What is the worst thing that could happen if Jim did follow his dreams? What would happen if he made a terrible mistake? Would he recover or would he become foolhardy and continue to do one silly thing after another?

As Jan answered my questions, the lights began to come on for her. She realized that she did have a basic trust in Jim. She knew he wouldn't become foolish, and she realized that a mistake or two wouldn't be nearly as detrimental to their relationship as what they were experiencing right now.

At this point, Jan was ready to look for new alternatives. She was ready to love and not to mother. I encouraged her to share his dreams. He needed to know that if it were possible, she would like to see him in a new job. He needed to know that she would buy him the sports car if she had the money. This step was hard, because she had been telling herself that if she didn't control him she would get hurt. She found, however, that as she gave him the responsibility to evaluate his own dreams, he controlled himself.

"As much as I want to," he said, "I really can't change jobs until we are on better financial footing." Jan breathed a sigh of relief. Jim felt closer to her now. He felt like she was on his side again. He felt understood.

Jan felt cared for again. She felt secure. She liked the way it made her feel to respect Jim again. Jan was even willing to consider working outside the home if it would help them to get where *they* wanted to be. Their marriage, which had almost died from smothering, was beginning to grow again. Balance in helping and encouraging is needed.

One caution: Don't help your spouse when he or she neither wants nor needs it. This is neither helpful nor loving; it's overindulgence. The message then is, "You're incapable" rather than "I love you." This is particularly important with a spouse who feels so inadequate that any task appears overwhelming. This spouse needs just enough help to see hope in his/her ability to complete the task. From there on the need is for encouragement and praise. It is important to remember that help is not taking over but rather assisting while he or she retains the primary responsibility for what is to be accomplished.[2]

The second type of smothering is doing things for people that they need to do for themselves.

Let's take a look at Mark and Susan's relationship. When they first got married, they did a lot of things together. They worked together, played together, worshiped together, cried together, and laughed together. They felt like one unit, but they each felt strong as individuals. You could hear the mutual admiration they had by the way they referred to each other. They were off to a great start.

When Susan became pregnant, Mark began to spoil her. He tried to do more of her work than he really should have. And she began to feel a little like a freeloader when she saw him over-extending himself.

Then the unexpected happened. Susan had a miscarriage. They were shaken to the core. Mark tried to care by doing, doing, doing. That only increased Susan's feelings of guilt and failure, and she began to withdraw into her shell. Mark tried to do more to help her get back on her feet. It didn't work. She did less. He did more. She felt worse! He felt worse.

One day Mark realized he wasn't just feeling worse. He was feeling ripped off. "She not only lets me do all the work," he said, "she doesn't even seem to know how bad I feel about the baby." Mark was doing it all, but he was developing some strange feelings toward Susan. At first he wouldn't even admit how empty and angry he felt. When I first suggested that he might be doing too much, he stared at me with unbelief. What I saw as smothering he saw as attempts at providing a life-support system.

"Why doesn't she do anything?" I asked.

"She can't," he said.

"Can't or doesn't have to?" I quizzed.

I pointed out that the best way to care for Susan was to help her feel competent again. This was never going to happen as long as Mark was feeding her dependence. He got the message and began to express his needs to her a little at a time. Instead of being quietly angry that his vest wasn't repaired on his favorite suit, he asked Susan to repair it. It took her a while to get started, but when she finally did they both felt better. Mark began to do less of Susan's normal responsibilities, and she began to pick them up again. At first it was because she had no choice. Later she recognized that she was feeling better as she was doing more. The smothering was over, and they began to get on with their life together.

Staying close to people without smothering is one of the most difficult challenges you may face. It is sometimes difficult to be helpful without being paternalistic or condescending. "I care" means "I want you to be all you can be, even if it means you may fall on your face at times. I love you too much to keep you in a body cast that weakens your muscles from lack of use."

Pat Answers

Have you ever received a right answer but to the wrong question? If so, you have experienced a pat answer.

A pat answer is a general belief or truth which on the surface seems to solve a problem. Most people I counsel have been victims of pat answer givers.

Sam was told, "What you need is just to trust the Lord."

True! Who doesn't need to trust the Lord more? The problem is Sam was trying with everything inside himself to trust the Lord, and nothing seemed to be happening. He felt God was a million miles away, and the pat answer only made him feel guilty, angry, and unloved by his pat answer friend.

A pat answer is usually a poor substitute for listening and understanding. We often assume we have the right answer before we have even heard the problem.

Jeanie tried to talk to her husband about a problem with a friend. Before she had even finished, Bill, her husband, said, "Your problem is that you just let her run over you all the time. You need to stand up for yourself."

Bill couldn't understand why Jeanie reacted to this statement by crying and running from the room. It was her pastor who finally found out how deeply she was hurt by Bill's pat answer. Jeanie had tried to stand up for herself. And it was not working.

Bill's pat answer had two drawbacks. It focused on his own agenda, not Jeanie's. It wasn't really caring at all. And Bill was trying to play psychologist. He believed he understood her and could read her mind. He didn't take the time to listen and treat her concerns as unique and special.

When people share concerns with you, try to understand their feelings and empathize with them. Don't tell them something they already know. Ask them what they have tried to do or what they would like to see happen. This leads the person beyond their turmoil toward some new possibilities for a solution.

Take the pat answer "Just trust God." Instead of telling a person to simply trust, I have found it helpful to ask him what he would like to be able to trust God for. If he can identify the area in which he wants to express faith, I can support him; I can pray for him; I can even coach him if I have had more experience trusting God in the area of struggle.

One of the reasons we rely too heavily on pat answers is that we have a desire to see problems solved instantly, with less pain. "Teach me patience, Lord. Now!"

When Sandy is in distress, I hurt as well. I want the perfect solution for her as quickly as possible. One problem sidesteps that answer: She is a very intelligent woman, and she has usually thought through all the pat answers I may generate. If I respond by giving her answers she has already tried or at least thought of, she may feel put down or belittled or not respected. I only add to her problem. But if I will listen and empathize, I may be just the encouragement she needs to keep up her search for a solution.

Encouragement and support are the opposite of pat answers. Sometimes we love people the most when we offer the fewest solutions. John Powell writes about what encouragement can really do for a person.

> One of the hardest-to-accept facts about true love is that
> it is liberating. Love offers a person roots (a sense of be-

longing) and wings (a sense of independence and freedom). What people really need is belief in themselves, confidence in their own ability to take on the problems and opportunities of life. This is what is meant by the second stage of love: encouragement. To en-courage means to put courage in. It instills into the recipient a new and fuller awareness of his or her own powers, strength, and self-sufficiency. Encouragement says, You can do it![3]

Encouragement will be discussed later as one of the tools of caring.

Pat answers may make the pat answer giver feel good with their appearance of helpfulness. But for the person in need, a handful of pat answers is only cruel and unusual punishment. Think how much better you feel when a friend listens to you and dialogues with you as you search for an answer. That's a whole world's difference from telling you what you should do and then condemning you when you are not able to follow through on the suggestion.

Even Scripture can be used as a pat answer. I have found that most people have more scriptural knowledge than they know what to do with. They need help in application. It is one thing to be told you need to forgive someone (a pat answer), but it is much harder to know how to forgive. I often ask people, "What do you think will have to happen in order for you to be able to forgive?" At first they may think I have a "canned" answer for them. Later they realize I want them to find the solutions for themselves. We are called to be examples and fellow travelers—not just dispensers of pat answers.

Conditional Caring

My family inconveniences me—if I want always to be able to give to them. Why do they often have needs at the times when I don't feel like giving? Why do they always want more or something different from what I am prepared to give?

My response to the inconvenience of caring is often to set conditions under which I will care. I may say, "Why don't we talk tomorrow?" or "As soon as you figure out what is bothering you, I will be happy to talk to you." Setting conditions such as these is not caring at all. These are self-protection devices which can harm others.

Demanding that people be a certain way is also a type of conditional caring. I may say to my wife, "If you were more submissive, I could be more loving." Even though this may be true, it is not a position that Scripture gives me the luxury of taking. Ephesians 5 doesn't have an "if" clause. I am called to love my wife as Christ loved the church, whether or not she is submissive. I am called to love her as myself, whether she makes me feel good or not. God sees caring through an unconditional lens.

Caring is best communicated by acceptance—acceptance which is not based on what others do for you. I feel loved when Sandy accepts me even when I have let her down. That loving response which I don't deserve frees me. John Powell has written eloquently about this.

> There is nothing else that can expand the human soul, actualize the human potential for growth, or bring a person into the full possession of life more than a love which is unconditional. We have labored for so long under the delusion that corrections, criticism, and punishments stimulate a person to grow. We have rationalized the taking out of our own unhappiness and incompleteness in many destructive ways. . . . Only recently have the behavioral sciences reached the point of enlightenment to show us that unconditional love is the only soil in which the seed of a human person can grow.[4]

Conditional caring usually demands a pay back. "I'll care for you as long as you give me what I need."

Demands cancel caring. When I demand that my wife do things for me, I deny her the opportunity to love me from her own free will. When I show friendship only in exchange for friendship, I don't even understand the meaning of the word "friend." Human fulfillment is not the result of bartering. It is the result of giving and receiving.

Expressing our wants or needs lets others know how to care for us. We should not eliminate "need" information; only demanding tones. I tell Sandy my needs, not because she must meet them, but so she can have the opportunity to meet the needs she can. When she can't or doesn't, I don't hold it against her. I know she wants to care and will as soon as she can. I have found this to be a refreshing alternative to the bitterness and demands which used to be more common in our relationship.

Friendships also need this freedom. Somehow we seem to get stuck in our childhood. "If you don't play with me, I won't be your friend." Sounds silly, doesn't it? It sounds even worse when you realize that the words are coming from your mouth.

Look for opportunities to care. Don't look for what you can get out of it. The more you look for return, the less return you will receive. Unconditional caring illustrates the great biblical truth that you have to lose your life to gain it. We cannot demand that others give us life, but we can give to see that their lives are enriched.

It is said that you cannot outgive each other. Try to outgive your spouse, your child, or your friend. It is a fantastic way to live! "God, why can't I live that way all the time?"

Caring from the Flesh

I was shocked the first time I realized that Galatians 6:7-8 referred to caring.

> Do not be deceived: God cannot be mocked. A man reaps what he sows. The one who sows to please his sinful nature, from that nature will reap destruction; the one who sows to please the Spirit, from the Spirit will reap eternal life (Galatians 6:7-8).

As I was growing up, I heard these verses many times. Yet they were always applied to sexual temptation and sexual sin. Imagine how surprised I was to read the verses in context. They refer to the way in which you might try to restore a brother to fellowship. The verses make clear that there is a way to relate to others which pleases our sinful nature and displeases God. And there is a way to care which follows the Spirit of God within us.

I understand from passages such as this that I may engage in a lot of caring behaviors which are aimed at serving me, not the other person. Caring for personal gain does not please God. Any time I hear a person say, "But honey, I only did it for your own good," there is a red flag raised in my mind. If you have to tell someone that it was for their own good, it is questionable that it was for their good. This publicly pronounced care may be only self-serving—showing up the other person in public or putting him down.

Caring from the flesh can usually be detected by asking yourself the following set of questions.

1. Do I really know the other person's needs?
2. Will my behavior lead to the satisfaction of one of their needs?
3. Would I be doing this for this person if no one knew about it?
4. Am I expecting something in return?
5. Am I able to serve the other person joyfully?

If your response to any of these five questions is no, you may be caring from the flesh. Why not take time to think through your motives until you come to a place where your caring is meaingful because it is God-directed? Why waste time caring from the flesh? You will only come away with a fat head and a flat heart.

Cleaning Up Your Act

What now? The worst thing you can do is to waste time worrying about past failures that root in nonproductive approaches to caring.

There is something you can do about today and its opportunities. Just as you may clean up a flowerbed in the spring of the year and plant new spring flowers, you can pull out one or more of the nonproductive approaches to caring and replace it with truly caring attitudes and actions. The chapters that follow will focus on productive approaches to help you on your caring journey.

Chapter 6, Notes

[1]Richard C. Nelson, *Choosing: A Better Way to Live* (Lake Park, Fla.: Guidelines Press, 1977), p. 92.

[2]Judson J. Swihart, *How Do You Say "I Love You"?* (Downers Grove, Ill.: InterVarsity Press, 1977), p. 32.

[3]John Powell, *Unconditional Love* (Niles, Ill.: Argus Communications, 1978), p. 86.

[4]Ibid, pp. 68, 69.

7

Identifying the Tools of Caring

**Desire is only the
place to start**

Recently I opened a two-pound can of coffee with a butter knife. At the risk of cutting off a few fingers as well as giving the butter knife a personal serated edge, I got into the coffee can. How much easier it would have been if I could have found a can opener.

When it comes to caring, each of us needs to find and use the right utensils to help without hurting ourselves or others. Caring is a complex process; a knowledge of what does work is essential. The following ten tools of caring will enable you to develop caring relationships.

Listening—The Basic Tool

All caring is based upon communication; there is no tool more important than the ability to listen. Listening helps you know the other person. In fact, the process of listening alone seems to meet one of man's basic needs—the need to be taken seriously.

Lack of caring in our society can be seen by the fact that we have a lot more talkers than we do listeners. Yet listening has a therapeutic power for many people. Listening reinforces feelings of self-worth and value.

When you listen, listen not only for the facts but for the feelings as well. The greatest problem with most people's listening skills is that they have learned to listen only for the purpose of giving a response. We listen only so we can talk.

When I listened to my wife in this manner, we barely had a relationship. She didn't feel that I cared for her. She felt that I was tolerating or patronizing her. Somewhere along the line I have begun to learn to listen to get to know her better. I have become as interested in my wife as I am in what she has to say. Sandy feels valued that I want to get to know who she is, what she feels, her dreams, her fears, and her frustrations. Listening goes beyond the facts to say, "Tell me who you are. I like what I have heard so far and I want to know more."

If you want to test your listening skills, tape record a few conversations with your spouse, your children, or your friends. Count the number of times you interrupt or change the conversation. Count the number of times you ask the person to tell you more. Observe when you were focused on your agenda as compared to the amount of time you stayed on track with the other person.

Make listening a priority. Turn off the TV. Throw away the newspaper or anything that distracts. And one final word. Learn to keep what you hear confidential. Don't be a gossip. All of us need to be able to pour out our hearts without worrying about whose ears our confessions will reach.

Understanding

I used to think that listening and understanding were the same. That's not true. You can't have understanding without listening; but listening alone will not insure understanding.

To understand is to see the world through the perspective of the other person. To understand is to share the feelings and ideas held by the other person. To understand is to walk in the other person's shoes or to sit in his place.

There was a time in my married life when I would have said that I understood perfectly the pressures my wife was feeling as the mother of several small children. Then Sandy became very ill, and I had to begin to assume some of the responsibility. It didn't take me long to realize that I not only didn't understand perfectly—I didn't understand at all! I began to wonder how she kept her sanity. I even began to wonder if I would be able to keep mine.

Here are some questions which may guide you in your efforts to understand:

1. What does this situation or event mean to this person?
2. What emotions is the person expressing?
3. How does this situation affect the person's view of self?
4. How does this situation affect the person's behavior?
5. What is this person telling himself about the situation?
6. Would this person like to talk more about the situation?
7. Am I willing to listen to understand rather than to give advice or fix it for the other person?

Understanding statements need to be simple and nondogmatic. For example: "It sounds like you are hurt and possibly angry" is better than "you are upset and angry and you just better straighten up." When both of you are aware that you are at least beginning to understand, it is good to ask what you might do to help. Leave the responsibility for identifying helpful actions to the one asking for help. His statements about what he needs may also add to your understanding.

Above all, don't force understanding. I once heard a mother of two lovely children speaking to a childless friend who had just had a miscarriage. The bereaved woman's face turned white then red with anger as the other stated, "Oh, I know exactly how you feel." Who can know? Who can understand? The best we can do is to try to identify with the person and be willing to learn more.

Persevering

It is not easy to learn. It is not easy to do . . . and keep on doing. If caring were easy, we would no doubt have more people stepping forth to care.

When you persevere, you stand by; you go the second mile. Hurting people often engage in love testing. They want to see if your love will last over time. Do you really want to understand, or are you just going through the motions? From childhood to old age, people ask the question, "Is there anyone who cares enough to stand by me?"

What do you say to someone who discredits your perseverance? What about this statement: "You only stuck with me out of obligation! You don't really care!"

I call this making crumbs. You are giving the person a cookie by staying close, and yet instead of receiving it, they crumble the gift and throw it back in your face. Hold the person responsible when this happens. Tell them you want to be with them, and that they are choosing to crumble the cookie. When they realize they are making crumbs, they will act more responsibly.

Perseverance gives a person time to process confusing thoughts or feelings. Confusion will make it difficult for a listener even to know how to help. That is when just being there helps.

There are times when Sandy has been so hurt or disappointed with herself that she cannot tell me what she needs. She may be aloof or nonresponsive; yet she needs me to stay close and reassure her of my love. Without forcing myself on her, without taking too much responsibility for her problem, without trying to fix it—I need simply to "stand by."

As you care for people they, like you, will fail repeatedly. And failure is where perseverance comes in handy. Success is rarely easy, and the path up the mountain is often marked by downhill skids.

Persevere with the person by helping him to keep his eyes on the goal. Show him ways in which he is progressing. Don't carry him, but allow him to rest against you as he regains his breath, strength, and courage.

Persevering is both emotional and physical. You believe in a person when he cannot believe in himself. You also are with the person physically, sometimes holding him, when he feels too weak to stand.

Encouraging

Just as we have too many talkers and not enough listeners, we also have too many criticizers and not enough encouragers. Ephesians 4:29-30 puts it on the line.

> Do not let any unwholesome talk come out of your mouths, but only what is helpful for building others up according to their needs, that it may benefit those who listen. And do not grieve the Holy Spirit of God, with whom you were sealed for the day of redemption (Ephesians 4:29-30).

What is encouragement, anyway? Listening is easy to grasp. It is an activity you carry out with a sense organ—your ear—plus your mind and emotions. Encouragement is not as simple. Sometimes listening is a form of encouragement. At other times, encouragement comes through talking or doing something. Encouragement depends upon the situation and the individual—both are unique every time encouragement is needed.

The tool of encouragement is forged by the tool of listening. Learn to hear what the person is saying. Then you may also be able to hear how you can encourage.

Despite the complexity of encouragement, there are some general qualities which form the basis for encouragement.

1. Acknowledge the other person's presence. It's hard to believe that many people think if they disappeared, no one would notice that they were missing. Remind people how nice it is to have them around.

2. Tell people how they are especially significant. For example, "You bring joy to me when you smile," or "You help me to understand myself better," or "You have talent."

3. Inform people you see growth taking place in them. All of us need to know that we are growing. We get discouraged when we feel that we are standing still. And it is hard to see your own progress.

4. Share the dreams. One of the things I appreciate most about my wife is the way in which she gets excited about my crazy ideas. Even when I am impractical, she doesn't squelch me. She dreams with me. As we dream together, my ideas may become clearer or we may revise them. I don't need to be told at the outset that my dream won't work. If that is true, time will teach me. The opportunity to dream is the important thing.

5. Support their activities. Whether a person faces a scary new activity or one of life's expected frightening chores, a friend or family member alongside supports the person through his times of doubt.

Encouragement, then, is a many-faceted tool. You can lend a helping hand, lead the cheers for success, and pass the kleenex after the failures. Next to listening, it is the most needed instrument in your caring toolbox.

Confrontation

Confrontation is the most misunderstood of all caring tools. The reason is quite clear. We normally confront only when we are angry; therefore we miss the caring in the midst of our confronting. David Augsburger has coined the term "care-fronting" to impress the need of holding people accountable in love.

Confronting is difficult. Our sinful nature causes us to be defensive toward another's input rather than receptive and teachable. I can learn a great deal from Sandy and my children if I am open to the "care-fronting" they offer me. Words chosen wisely and questions selected carefully will do a lot to take the edge off of the defensive.

As a young Bible school student, I remember being confronted by an older student who was my friend. He asked one question which caused me to change some things in my life. "Is this behavior getting the results that you want?" If he had told me that I was on the wrong track and that I needed to shape up, I might not have accepted his counsel. However, his loving question was received and prompted me to discover for myself the areas no one but I could change.

Galatians 6:1-5 stresses the importance of your attitude when you seek to care through confrontation. Notice these important phrases: "restore him gently," "watch yourself," "carry each other's burdens." Allow this passage of Scripture to sink in about your attitudes during confrontation.

The unanswered question in confrontation is, "When?" I have a tendency to confront to meet my own needs. When I confront to meet my needs, it is usually to relieve tension or to let off steam through anger. Genuine confrontation in love comes from a sincere heart that refuses to let the other person be less than he can be.

If I confront in love, the timing will not always be convenient. It may have to be immediate and last longer than a few minutes. David W. Johnson has carefully spelled out the need for time if you are to be helpful through confrontation.

> Do not "hit and run." Confront only when there is time
> to define the conflict jointly and schedule a negotiating
> session. A confrontation is the beginning of a negotiat-
> ing process, not an end in itself. Thus, confrontations
> are not to be confused with hit-and-run events in which

one person gives his views of, and feelings about, a conflict and then disappears before the other person can respond. Hit-and-run tactics tend to escalate conflicts in negative directions and build resentment and anger in the victims. An important aspect of confrontation is timing. Always be sure that enough time exists to discuss the conflict before confronting another person.[1]

Confrontation is often best done in a family when the level of emotion is low. When I am upset, I may not be receptive to confrontation. I am probably already confronting myself and incurring unruly emotions. When I have calmed down, my wife can approach me to confront me and find a willing, though not eager, listener.

One caution needs to be stated. Do not put off "care-fronting" forever just to avoid conflict. Remember, it is a responsibility of love, though an uncomfortable one.

Here are some basic rules which may help.

1. Be factual, not accusatory.

2. Convey the value you see in the other person.

3. Seek to identify with the other person's feelings.

4. Avoid threatening terms such as, "If you don't stop, I'll . . ."

5. Avoid faulty generalizations such as, "You always," or "You never."

6. Seek feedback from the other person. Allow him to tell you how he is doing with your confrontation.

7. Help the other person to identify some ways he might want to change.

8. Try to generate responsibility, not guilt.

9. Ask the person how you might help him in his efforts to grow in the area confronted.

10. Pray for and follow up with the person.

Responding to a challenge to change can be very lonely. The person you confront needs to know that you are still there. Remember, your responsibility is to help the other person to be all he can be.

Comforting

There are two things that many people do not seem to know how to do. The first is giving comfort. The second is re-

ceiving comfort. Obviously, the two are related. Second Corinthians 1:3-4 offers us a starting place in correcting this defi-
cit.

> Praise be to the God and Father of our Lord Jesus Christ,
> the Father of compassion and the God of all comfort,
> who comforts us in all our troubles, so that we can com-
> fort those in any trouble with the comfort we ourselves
> have received from God (2 Corinthians 1:3-4).

The order of actions in these verses seems very important.
We are to receive comfort from God so we can comfort others
who are in need. We must first *receive* so we may *give*.

Many people will say, "I have never been comforted by
God!" This belief and very real feeling runs contrary to Scripture. The passage quoted above states that "God . . . comforts us in our trials." If this verse is true, then why have we
not felt comforted?

I believe I have at least a partial answer. When I am hurt or
in trouble, I tend to look away from God. I become very narrow, and I even begin to define what I will accept as comfort.
In this frame of mind I overlook the comfort God is giving. If I
am looking for comfort only in a round box, and God chooses
to send it in a shoe box, I will miss it. Despondency results
from blaming Him for not caring. It is a terrible trap.

There is a second way that I may miss God's comfort. I
sometimes have trouble translating physical words from the
pages of Scripture. I know intellectually that God comforts,
but I don't always feel it. When our children were small and
were afraid, they wanted physical comfort. They didn't want
to be told that they would be all right. They wanted to feel
Sandy or me.

With whose arms or hands does God comfort?

The passage cited above states that God is the God of all
comfort. It then states that we are vehicles of comfort. In
other words, we put into human form the comfort of God.
What an awesome responsibility! No wonder people do not
feel comforted if we as a body are not sharing the comfort of
Christ.

In the practical sense, then, how do we care by comforting?
I believe comforting has four major elements.

1. Identifying with the loss the person feels.

2. Standing beside the person so that they won't have to experience their sorrow alone.

3. Helping them to search for hope.

4. Encouraging them in the rebuilding process.

What does it mean to identify with another person's loss? To me it means that you accept the loss without trying to minimize it or sweep it under the rug. Too often we try to make people feel better too soon. They don't need quick solutions. They need patient hope.

The second step in comforting is standing by the person. Be available but do not be pushy. Ask him what his needs are and be willing to wait until he is able to answer.

Assisting in the search for hope is a third part of the comforting process. The person has tunneled down to despair; he cannot be left there. When my father was about to die, I remember his physician saying, "Well, we always try to leave a little room for hope." I was comforted.

We should not always feel that we must spell out the hope for the person. This is a mistake. You may help him to see some possibilities, but he must discover the hope for himself if it is to be life-changing. A few suggested directions, a gentle reminder of God's faithfulness, and a bright hope that he will indeed make it is what is needed—not a pushiness toward something he can't quite believe. Remember that you yourself will need guidance to perform this important caring task.

Finally, encourage the person. One who is sorrowing has trouble seeing that he is helping himself—or others.

You can be the one who points to successes and helps the person see his progress. Your encouragement can level out the ups and downs of starting over. To comfort is to give hope. Polish this important tool of caring.

Problem Solving

There is something basic to the make-up of man that wants to solve problems. We live in a very complex society, one which has been marred by man's humanity. One of the effects of sin has been to leave us with many problems which seem unsolvable. Paul Welter refers to these situations as predicaments.

If a girl is baking a triple batch of cookies, she may seek help from her mother in getting the measurements right. This is a *problem* situation because another person can give helpful advice or directions. A predicament, on the other hand, suggests a difficult situation offering *no* satisfactory solution. Another important difference is that a predicament is characterized by uniqueness, rather than by the commonality that characterizes a problem. A person who is in a predicament is alone in that situation. No one else's situation is exactly like his, at least not from his point of view.[2]

Giving a person advice to solve a problem may be a short term act of caring. But caring for a person caught in a predicament requires a commitment to stay on for encouragement. Consider your own needs when you want, but can't find, a solution. You try to enlist the help of others, but soon you become discouraged by their quick advice. The greatest skill in problem solving is not giving advice but rather giving encouragement. I have been impressed with Proverbs 18:24 in this regard. "A man of many companions may come to ruin, but there is a friend who sticks closer than a brother."

I often receive advice from my companions, but the friend who sticks closer than a brother is the one I find helpful when I am facing predicaments. It is this friend who can usually stand by me in my time of need.

There are several specific aspects of problem solving which you may wish to consider building into your repertoire of caring behaviors.

1. Listen carefully to help the person clearly see all sides of the picture. Draw him out. Ask him to explain the situation again or from another perspective. He may be stuck with a narrow view which your questions can help to reveal.

2. Help the person say where he would like to be. Too often people just want things to be different without saying how they would like them to be different.

3. Help the person search for possibilities. Once he says where he would like to be, you may help him see some paths to that destination. Let him do the work. You are not the pilot. He is. You should serve as a navigator who keeps the flight on course.

This is especially true as you try to care for your spouse who is caught in a predicament. He needs to search for solutions himself. If you take too active a role in fixing the situation, the person will never realize his own abilities or God's faithfulness to him.

My wife is excellent when it comes to helping me or others sort through predicaments. She keeps a positive attitude, provides encouragement, and stimulates me to think of new possibilities. She has learned not to try to put the lid on before the solution or possible solutions are in the can.

4. Help the person evaluate the possibilities he discovers. Ask him to enumerate the pros and cons of each possibility. Ask him how each possible solution matches up with his values and his total view of himself as a person. Ask him which possibilities he can live with. Remember. He must decide because he has to live with the consequences.

5. Remember that deciding is only half of the battle. It is sometimes easier to make a decision than it is to implement the decision. After the person has decided, your caring role may become one of supporting him or holding him accountable or both as he puts his new ideas into practice. Don't be afraid to tell the person that you will be praying for him and that you will check back in two or three days to see how he is progressing. Awareness of your prayers and continuing concern may help him to overcome some of the temptation to avoid the problem.

Problem solving skills as viewed in the manner I have presented them may seem formal and not very caring. What we must realize is that problems are very much a part of our lives, and we need to care for each other in this area. It is a part of the total package.

Modeling

One of the very real side effects of the breakdown in the family has been the loss of opportunity to see people model success in intimate relationships. Children often do not have the privilege of seeing their parents model how to get along. The parents couldn't get along so they split. Unfortunately, many follow this same model and the problem continues from generation to shattered generation.

We have found that just modeling peace and quietness is a great help to people who haven't seen any model other than shouting and violence. Don't try to force the person into your mold but ask the question, "How would you feel if you were able to do . . . ?" Or state, "I find it helpful to do . . ."

In many ways your words may be unimportant. It is your actions which will get the person's attention. He will watch how you relate to him and will try to follow your example as he seeks to care for others. In 1 Timothy 4:12 Paul writes: "Don't let anyone look down on you because you are young, but set an example for the believers in speech, in life, in love, in faith and in purity."

There are days when you will not feel very competent as a model for others. You may feel you need help rather than being able to give help. Nothing says you can't have bad days. Even being transparent about your struggle may be a help to someone who is looking for a model about dealing with struggling. People do watch us. We have no choice but to be the best model we can be. Can you see this as an opportunity rather than a threat? Realize, too, that God is highly interested in your success. You are not alone in your modeling.

Acting For

Our emphasis to this point has been upon the tools of caring which are passive and supportive. We have placed a heavy premium on facilitating the growth of others by standing with them, helping them to be all they can be. There are, however, times when you help those who cannot help themselves. Your strengths must become their strength until they become stronger themselves. In other words, there are times when the caring person stops asking, "Is there anything I can do?" and begins to do the obvious.

Couples need to learn that there are times when love and caring need to be expressed in helping hands. Young mothers particularly need physical help. Busy husbands need assistance with those parts of their lives that begin to pile up. Lifting a burden can go a long way toward helping the person to regain hope.

Look for opportunities to care for people by acting on their behalf. They may be reluctant at first to receive your help, but if the need is there, be persistent. I care means "I want to help you do what you cannot at this point in time do for yourself."

Joe brought his wife Lenor back to his small hometown of Tracy, California, where they had a three-hundred acre farm. Joe's friends and neighbors were mainly farmers.

Just before planting time, Lenor had to have her leg amputated. Joe took her to Mayo Clinic in Minnesota, where they stayed for almost a month. Happy as they were with her good recovery, the young couple were discouraged because as they rode home they had lost their chance for a crop that year.

Their sadness turned to smiles when they arrived home. Friends and neighbors had not only been "praying for Lenor," but the whole town of Tracy had turned out to plow and plant their three-hundred acres. For good measure, the town had also landscaped their front yard.

Joe and Lenor had friends who cared.[3]

Giving Space

In general, caring behaviors involve moving toward or alongside the other person. There are times, however, when you need to be sensitive to a person's need to be alone.

It takes time to integrate new thoughts and feelings into your life. As a friend, you may help the other person get started in the process—but you cannot do it for him. Be sensitive to those times when you need to withdraw.

Withdrawal is not to be confused with abandonment. If I withdraw from Sandy to give her time to process her thoughts or feelings, she needs to know that I will be back to stand beside her again. It is also important to withdraw in response to the needs of the other person, not just your needs.

Sometimes I must withdraw for a period of time to restore my ability to care more fully. This has its place. Too often people give space only when they are angry. By mutual agreement through prayerful discernment, you can learn when to give people breathing room and when to step in and provide artificial respiration. Both are needed at times.

Putting It All Together

The key to caring is to realize that these tools of caring are provided by God as His means of loving others through us.

He will sharpen our tools.

Caring is God's business. He will specially develop you as a caring person. And He will uniquely combine these tools with others to help you care for others with "the comfort we ourselves have received from God."

Chapter 7, Notes

[1]David W. Johnson, *Reaching Out*, 2nd ed. (Englewood Cliffs, NJ: Prentice-Hall, Inc., 1981), p. 231.

[2]Paul Welter, *Family Problems and Predicaments: How to Respond* (Wheaton, Ill.: Tyndale, 1977), p. 26.

[3]Muriel James and Louis Savary, *The Heart of Friendship* (New York: Harper & Row, 1978), pp. 79-80.

8

Sharpening
Your
Tools

**Practice doesn't make perfect—
only better**

WhEN I WAS a boy, I shared the burning ambition of many other boys growing up in America . . . becoming a major league baseball player.

My father helped to kindle that fire in my young soul. Even though he was past thirty when I was born, he always awed me with his skills in the game. I can close my eyes right now and see him belting a home run at a community picnic game. I can see his smile as he crossed home plate, surrounded by a dozen cheering men.

As young as I was, I knew they recognized Dad's skill—and envied him for it. Naturally, Dad and I played a lot of catch over the years. He would even pitch to me after he had worked hard in the fields all day. During all of those times of play, however, Dad kept stressing two important lessons to me:

Learn to do it right.

Practice until it becomes automatic.

He told me about the hours he had spent throwing a rubber ball against the barn strengthening his arm, increasing his speed, honing his aim. That impressed me. "Practice may not make you perfect," he would tell me, "but it sure makes you better." Dad may not have been a major leaguer, but in my book he was a baseball genius and I learned a great deal from him.

There Are No Experts in the Field

Unfortunately, it's much easier to find expert instruction in baseball or tennis or hockey than it is in the vitally important realm of caring. You can go to most bookstores and find a host of books on sports fundamentals but you would have to search long and hard to find a volume that says, "Here's how to care for your spouse. Here's how you can become a more caring friend." In fact, caring is such a unique and individualized subject that I dare say there *are no experts* in the field.

When Sandy and I put on caring seminars we take pains to stress that we are not "experts"—just fellow learners. We can suggest some tools, some methods, and some helpful ideas but expertise in caring must come from personal practice—not books or seminars. You become a more caring person as you select some of the tools and then begin to use them—over and over again.

My friend Jim did just that. He knew that he wasn't doing a very good job of meeting Nancy's needs but he was willing to learn. I encouraged him to focus on one skill at a time and Jim chose the hardest one of all . . . listening. After several weeks of excruciating work—and some encouraging progress—Jim acknowledged that he had probably never listened to anyone before in his entire life. His thing had always been talking, and when he couldn't do that he just drifted off by himself. "It's no wonder Nancy has so much anger inside," he said. "I never gave her a chance to work any of it off as it came up."

Jim is not a perfect listener now but Nancy would tell you with a twinkle in her eye that he is certainly better than he was. His practice is paying off. He won't be giving any public seminars on the subject, but he will be giving his ear to Nancy and the children. And as much as he may try to make you think otherwise, he is beginning to enjoy it.

Most Caring Skills Are Learned by Trial and Error

Have you ever admired a friend's skills so much that you resolved to imitate them in a given area? If you have, you probably learned something about that process. *It doesn't work.* Sure, your friend might have some real skills and great ideas, but after some painful trial and error you'll most likely have to do it your way—not your friend's way.

My friend Royce is one of the world's greatest hosts. Every time Sandy and I went to their home we came away impressed. Being in his home was helpful to me and I resolved to be more like him. The problem was, I couldn't pull it off. He was a different person with a different set of guests. Through trial and error, however, I learned how to adapt some of his hospitality skills into our own social times. Royce had inspired me, but I needed to find the way that was best for the Wilsons.

The same trial and error process is necessary in caring. You have to learn how to do it your way. But I would add this caution: Caring isn't caring unless it is received by the other person. You may practice some caring behaviors which feel good to you, but do not meet the needs of your spouse or friend. If this is the case, try again. It may take several starts but sooner or later you will come to the place where others' needs are being met and you are feeling good about yourself in the process.

Sandy tried again and again, in several different ways, to care for me by encouraging me in my public speaking. Somehow, however, it seemed that her efforts always fell short of the mark. She would state both her positive and negative reactions. Unfortunately, many times I could hear only the negative. I would get defensive and she would get discouraged. I'm glad to say that even though she was discouraged she didn't give up. Now she is a constant source of encouragement to me in this area. I finally began to be able to hear the positive which made the negative less threatening. It took many trials and many errors but her practice has paid off—to my great joy and gratitude.

Take the Risk Until You Become More Skilled

Sandy's caring for me in the area of my speaking illustrates the need for trial-and-error learning. It also shows the value of taking risks—even in the face of failure—until those caring skills begin to bear fruit. Caring is like learning to speak a foreign language. You will make mistakes and you will be embarrassed. It is nice to know, however, that even when you are in the process of making the mistakes you are also

communicating your care. It is, after all, better to say something with halted or unpolished speech than not to speak at
all. The language of caring is often a non-verbal language that
says he or she cared enough to try.

Jennifer didn't really know how to reach out to Tom. She
knew that he was hurting because of things that were going
on at the office. Each time that she spoke to him all she got
was anger. It hurt—badly—but she didn't give up. Finally a
simple phrase unlocked the door. "I really don't want to pry
or anger you, Tom," she said, "but I'm trying to tell you I am
on your side." At that Tom broke down and shared that he
felt trapped. He felt like he had to do it all alone without the
help of anyone and yet at the same time was afraid to fail and
desperately afraid to be alone. Suddenly he had found the
friend he needed. He had rediscovered his helpmate.

Taking risks is even more difficult when you have tried and
been rebuffed. You have probably had this experience if you
are married or have been involved in a close friendship. That
old cliché is true . . . we really do hurt the ones we love. And
it takes courage to stay close enough to be hurt again. The
irony of the whole matter is that staying close enough to get
hurt again will also keep you close enough to be helpful and
caring. It is often a nothing ventured, nothing gained situation. Paul seems to have understood this process when he
wrote about love.

> It is not rude, it is not self-seeking, it is not easily
> angered, it keeps no record of wrongs. Love does not
> delight in evil but rejoices with the truth (1 Corinthians
> 13:5-6).

When we get hurt by our spouse, family members, or
friends, we may need to let them know that we have been
hurt—but not hold it over their heads. So often we feel that if
we tell our friends that we have been hurt they will change
immediately. Such is not the case. Change comes slowly. It
will occur as we expose ourselves to the risk of repeated hurts
even as our friends learn to express their needs and accept
our care. Caring requires dependent persistence: dependence upon God to protect us from the bitterness of being repeatedly hurt and persistence to perform the caring deeds
which God reveals to us.

Go Over the Same Ground Until You Get It Right

One of the most difficult things for me to do early in our married life was to compliment Sandy. It wasn't that I was blind to her beauty or talents, I just wasn't used to saying things the way she needed to hear them. My compliments always seemed to have a hook, or lack that ring of genuineness. My wording was often inept and awkward. I remember wanting to tell her how nice her hair looked; what I *said* was "your hair isn't as straggly as it used to be." I loved her so much and yet communicated it so poorly. Once we got past the hurts and counter-hurts, I began to learn some better ways to express my feelings. I went over the same ground many times and we talked about the types of compliments that she could really receive. In the process, I learned that the problem was not all mine. She had to accept some responsibility for hearing what I was saying. The more we talked about it, the more skill we found. Bitterness turned to sweetness and she began to receive my caring support and to support me in my attempts to care. I would be lying if I said that this happened in one or two or even ten attempts. As a matter of fact, we still find ourselves going back over the same old ground sometimes. Practice hasn't made perfect, but it has made better. We feel more positive about each other now because each of us cares enough to hang in there.

Sometimes we mistakenly feel we are caring for people. Jim wanted to lighten his wife's responsibilities so he began to help her with the dishes. He was surprised when she seemed more frustrated than helped.

One day he said, "I'm trying to help you. Why are you getting angry with me?"

"It's not that I don't appreciate your help," she said. "It's just that I can't find the dishes when you put them away."

Luckily, Jim was able to say, "If that's the problem, let me wash and you can put the dishes away where you can find them."

The point is simply this: Get feedback from the people you'd like to care for. Ask them to tell you what things you do that are helpful. This is difficult at first, but as you see the quality of your caring improve you will be glad you asked. No one really wants to waste their caring efforts or practice the wrong behaviors. You may gather the courage to ask what things you do which *do not* seem to be helpful. This, of course, is more difficult. If you want people to be honest, you have to be prepared to accept their honest criticism. I have found that I can accept criticism if I view it as an opportunity to learn rather than as evidence of past failures. Doing something in the past that was ineffective doesn't mean failure. I'd rather call it a stepping stone on the way to effectiveness.

There is a second type of feedback that can help you monitor your growth in caring. This is feedback from friends or family who are close observers. Tell them what you are trying to do for others and ask them how you are coming across. These observations—coming from an outside, more objective source—may be extremely valuable. Sandy and I have found this a helpful way to check on our caring skills with our children. I may be frustrated with an interaction I have had with one of the children and I will go to Sandy for input. I usually tell her what I was trying to do and then ask her to tell me what I did that seemed to be helpful and what seemed to be counter-productive. I am not always able to take advantage of her input because I may be too tender to receive it. However, when I am able to ask, it is usually helpful.

A third way to learn how you come across is to check your own tracks. Fear of failure often prevents us from looking back to see where we have been. This is unfortunate because we can learn so much by trying to objectively evaluate what we do. Look carefully at the reactions you get from people. You can learn to read people's responses. If what you do doesn't accomplish what you want, try another way. Don't change completely. It is often the subtle changes that make the difference. As one popular western writer puts it, "keep an eye out on your backtrail."

Separate Your Needs from Those of Your Spouse or Friend

Much of what we do in life is governed by our own needs. This is true even when we feel we are doing something just for the sake of the other person. Whether we like to admit it or not, we tend to do the things that meet our needs. This is one of the reasons Galatians 6:1-10 contains a strong warning against trying to restore a brother (a caring thing to do) in the wrong attitude.

> Do not be deceived: God cannot be mocked. A man
> reaps what he sows. The one who sows to please his sin-
> ful nature, from that nature will reap destruction; the
> one who sows to please the Spirit, from the Spirit will
> reap eternal life. Let us not become weary in doing
> good, for at the proper time we will reap a harvest if we
> do not give up. Therefore, as we have opportunity, let
> us do good to all people, especially to those who belong
> to the family of believers (Galatians 6:7-10).

When I have tried to reach out to someone I have found it helpful to ask myself why I did what I did. Sometimes I realize that I really did it for me, not him. This is not always bad. Sometimes I do things for me which are caring for the other person. The danger comes when I do things for me and don't really evaluate whether the things care for the other person or not.

Sandy and I have found it helpful to our relationship to discuss this point quite openly. My mind flashes to "the case of the shopping spree." Going shopping with Sandy is a loving thing for me to do. If, however, I go only to control her spending I may be meeting my needs rather than hers. In that case, I've not helped our relationship at all. If I'm really concerned about caring for her, I need to carefully evaluate my motives.

Sandy faces this struggle, too. She may turn to me while we're shopping and ask, "Do you like this dress?" This is a potentially dangerous question. On the surface, it appears to be a caring behavior. She seems to be communicating that she values my opinion. What happens, however, if she argues with that opinion and tries to convince me that I am wrong? At that point it is obvious that her needs have become more important than mine. If both of us follow these artificial methods of "caring," our learning will be limited to improved fighting techniques.

Sometimes when my opinion is asked but not received, I may follow up with a question such as, "What is your purpose in buying the dress?" If she says, "for work," I will usually say, "Buy the one that helps you to feel the most confident. You look fine in either one." If she says, "I want to buy it for you," I will say, "Buy that one. It is the one I like for me." This type of interaction was difficult at first. But by learning to interact in this way we're both beginning to feel "heard." We are beginning to sort and separate our individual needs from the needs of the other. This, too, takes practice. As you learn to resist the temptation to wallow in hurt feelings you will learn to meet the needs of your spouse or your friend.

Reading Books and Watching Caring People

My father—besides being a baseball genius—is a caring man. Recently he stayed with us for two weeks and it was a joy to watch him in action. This time, however, I made it a point to take specific note of his caring ways. I listened carefully to his words and observed his thoughtful actions. This was a delight for me because I was able to see refined in him some of the caring behaviors which I am just now trying to perfect. I told him so, too. I let him know how much I appreciate the things he has taught me.

If you want to learn how to care, watch people who are successful at caring. Scripture not only tells us to imitate Christ, it also urges us to observe and imitate the behavior of those who are successful followers of Christ. "Whatever you have learned or received or heard from me, or seen in me," said the apostle Paul, "put it into practice" (Philippians 4:9a).

The man from Tarsus is offering practical counsel—advice you can plug into your life *today*. Right now pause and select someone whom you recognize to be a caring person. Determine that you will watch that person and try some of the caring things he does. As we mentioned already, some of the things he does won't work for you because you are two different people. That's okay! There will be other things that you can learn from him which will give you a real sense of fulfillment. And those are things you need to practice and perfect.

Allow me to add one word of caution at this point. Don't prejudge the caring actions you observe before you have tried them for yourself. If you prejudice yourself, you may decide against trying some things that might prove extremely fulfilling for yourself and others. For instance, I used to think sending a card to my wife or a friend was silly. What a waste, I thought! One day, however, after I saw how much Sandy enjoyed a card from a friend, I decided to try it. To my amazement, I found that she was overjoyed by that simple little act. And—as much as I hated to admit it—I'd really had a good time picking it out for her. It was a time of savoring how much

Sandy means to me. I am now a regular card shopper and sender and I am beginning to enjoy receiving them. In other words, try it—you may like it!

Reading books is another way to learn new ways to care. Fortunately, the shelves of bookstores are filled with helpful books. You have to look carefully, because some of the best books on caring may not even contain the word "caring." They may say "listening" or "loving" or "affirming" or "communication." Pick up a book or two and take the time to read them. Then *practice* some of the things you read. See if they work for you. You may find some new ideas which will revolutionize your ability to care.

I would especially encourage men to try to get some ideas by observing others or by reading. Men usually don't receive much reinforcement on this concept of caring for others. I've had many men confide to me in my office that they know next to nothing about it. Read a book or watch a friend, men. Caring can change your life! If you have read this far, your life may be in the process of change.

Step into the Gap

Hebrews 11:6a contains one of the inescapable truths of Scripture: ". . . and without faith it is impossible to please God. . . ." God has chosen to make faith a prerequisite to learning many of the skills He wants us to have. If you want to learn to care, you must believe that God can and will teach you to care. As the rest of the verse says, ". . . because anyone who comes to him must believe that he exists and that he rewards those who earnestly seek him." If you earnestly want to care and trust God to teach you to be a caring person, you may be assured that He will do so. Not instantly. Not without self-examination. Not without effort on your part. But He will teach you in this area if you are willing to believe Him and then "step into the gap." What does that mean? The concept is presented graphically in figure 8.1.

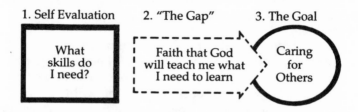

Figure 1: Skill Acquisition and Faith

The biblical principle for this concept is found in Philippians.

> Not that I have already obtained all this, or have already
> been made perfect, but I press on to take hold of that for
> which Christ Jesus took hold of me. Brothers, I do not
> consider myself yet to have taken hold of it. But one
> thing I do: Forgetting what is behind and straining to-
> ward what is ahead, I press on toward the goal to win
> the prize for which God has called me heavenward in
> Christ Jesus (Philippians 3:12-14).

Forget the past, Paul tells us. Get your eyes off your own
inadequacies and press toward that prize with everything
you've got. It is only when we press toward the prize—stepping into the gap by faith—that we experience God's enable-
ment. Although many things seem "too difficult" for us to
learn, we are not limited to our natural strengths! It is God
who equips us for the service He wants us to perform,
whether it is teaching a class, preaching a sermon, loving the
unlovely, or caring for others as we've never cared before. He
wants to teach us the joy of giving even a cup of cold water in
His name. (See Mark 9:41.)

Many times when Sandy and I encourage clients to trust
God for new ways to care for each other we hear them say,
"It's just too hard. I can't do it!" I find myself wanting to
shout, *who says valuable skills are easy to attain? Who says life has
to be easy?* You will never learn who God really is until you
trust Him to meet you at the point of your needs. Just because
you and I don't like to learn difficult things doesn't mean that
God is not good or that life should be different. Difficult tasks
provide us with some of the greatest opportunities for faith
and growth. This is reality. This is something we must face.
Paul Hauck speaks strongly to this point.

Before you can discipline yourself to overcome an un-
pleasant state of affairs, you will first have to accept the
fact that reality must be faced. To go on a diet, to get up
early to go to work, to speak in front of a large group of
people are specific examples. It does you no good whatever to insist pigheadedly that you should not have to
get up early in the morning, that you should have been
given the gift of gab so that you would not be nervous
before an auditorium full of people, and that nature
made a big mistake when it made people with a tendency to get fat.

All these statements make no sense whatever, because there is no reason why the world should be any
different from what it is. You are simply behaving like a
child if you go around stating that because you don't
like the world, it has to be different.[1]

Stepping into the gap and learning new caring skills *is*
hard. And without the dimension of faith you will be shocked
by your human limitations. But with faith, you will be pro-
pelled by God-given possibilities. It is up to you and me how
we are going to live. Which way will we choose?

Chapter 8, Notes

[1]Paul Hauck, *How to Do What You Want to Do* (Philadelphia: Westminster Press, 1976), pp. 26-27.

9

Helping
Others
to Care

Encourage one another to
love and good deeds

THE OLDER I GET the more I am convinced that God made us to be dependent on one another. I'm not talking about an unhealthy dependency—all "take" and no "give." I am talking about the type of dependency that is stressed in the book of Romans.

> For by the grace given me I say to every one of you: Do not think of yourself more highly than you ought, but rather think of yourself with sober judgment, in accordance with the measure of faith God has given you. Just as each of us has one body with many members, and these members do not all have the same function, so in Christ we who are many form one body, and each member belongs to all the others. We have different gifts, according to the grace given us. If a man's gift is prophesying, let him use it in proportion to his faith. If it is serving, let him serve; if it is teaching, let him teach; if it is encouraging, let him encourage; if it is contributing to the needs of others, let him give generously; if it is leadership, let him govern diligently; if it is showing mercy, let him do it cheerfully (Romans 12:3-8).

We are all charged with the responsibility of using our gifts for the sake of other Christians. In addition, God uses us to teach and sharpen other believers. Most people who are not caring people don't care because they don't know how. God wants us to stimulate each other to develop caring skills—to encourage one another to be all that we can be in this realm of our lives. I have noted that as I strive to teach others to become more caring, my own caring skills are sharpened in the process. Let's look at some specific things you can do to help others develop their ability to care for family and friends.

Modeling: If You Really Want to Teach Me, Show Me

Sandy and I have had the privilege of having many university students in our home. We've often marveled at the comments they make as they leave our home. One said, "I just love to watch how you and Sandy relate! I've never had the opportunity to see a Christian marriage in action before." Another said, "You make it look like fun, not something to be dreaded."

We feel awkward at times like these—we know that we have so many things to learn. On the other hand, we are thankful to God for teaching us some things that are improving our ability to care for each other. We are committed to living our lives as openly as we can. Both of us treasure the hope that God will use some of the things He is teaching us to help someone else become more caring.

Frankly, it isn't always fun to be an example. This is especially true when you feel you have been a *bad* example. But if our lives can be used to challenge or encourage another person, this is joy! What better way could be found to teach than to serve as a model? Sometimes Sandy and I model genuine success. But we also model recovery following failure. An effective model needs—above all—to be real. Don't hide behind perfection. Let people see your strengths and your weaknesses. People can learn from both.

Let me suggest some specific types of modeling.

1. *Model kind words.* The Bible says a soft answer turns away wrath (Proverbs 15:1). Caring is best conveyed when the volume is moderate. In my counseling sessions I frequently ask, "What would happen if you were to say something like 'Bill, I know how you feel but I don't know how to deal with my own anger'?" Almost every time the person will say, "Well, in the first place I could never say it in that calm a voice. When I am angry I shout!" I always tell them to try the new way. Just because you haven't been able to be calm or

kind in the past doesn't mean that you can't do it now.

2. *Model the actions that speak louder than words.* Do kind, caring things and others will learn caring and kindness by watching you. Sometimes it even gets contagious. Don't *tell* your children how to be kind, *show* them—by being kind to them. One action is often worth a thousand lectures. Scripture challenges us, ". . . set an example for the believers in speech, in life, in love, in faith and in purity" (1 Timothy 4:12b).

3. *Model rationality.* Be a responder, not a reactor. A reactor usually reacts from the emotions. If you say something negative about me and I react, I will usually get defensive or angry. If I am a responder, however, I will think about what you have said. I'll take some time to decide what is true and what is false. When I have thought things through I am in a better position to care for you, and for you to care for me. Reacting is usually counterproductive. It pays to take time and mull things over. After they overcome their amazement, your spouse, your family members, and friends will appreciate—and want to emulate—your model of thoughtful calmness. If you fail initially, get a hold of yourself as soon as you can. It is never too late to be calm and thoughtful.

4. *Model vulnerability.* Throughout this book we have suggested that people are reluctant to show caring because they are afraid of being hurt. If we are going to help people to become more caring, we need to show them that we can become vulnerable—and still survive. I have tried to model vulnerability for my children. Although they have not always understood, they have often responded with love and a desire to be close. It is hard for me to admit to them that I have handled situations wrongly. It's tough to come right out and say, "Listen, I was thinking of my own needs more than yours." When I am vulnerable, however, we usually end up on the same side of the problem. From there we can work together to find a solution. Admitting your faults can be a very caring thing to do.

5. *Model forgiveness.* Homes and churches are being—literally—torn apart today by lack of forgiveness. There are just too many people with long blacklists. Blacklists create distance and make caring harder. I am afraid to take the risk of caring when a failure could put me on someone's blacklist. To

forgive means that I no longer choose to view you though the lens of your sin. I choose to set the offense aside and to see you without the distortion. "I forgive" means "I choose to believe that you are interested in my well-being rather than hurting me again. I will give you a fresh start—free and clear." Forgiveness is the pinnacle of caring for others, but it is also a caring thing to do for yourself. Unforgiving people are bitter people.

> Get rid of all bitterness, rage and anger, brawling and slander, along with every form of malice. Be kind and compassionate to one another, forgiving each other, just as in Christ God forgave you (Ephesians 4:31-32).

Point Out Potential

Knowing yourself is one of the most difficult tasks of life. Many people never attain this goal. How do you know if you are a caring person? Sometimes you know by the reactions you get. At other times, however, the feedback is too vague or too mixed to sort out. We can help one another in this regard. As you observe your family and friends, take note of the caring behaviors you see exhibited. Then let them know about it. Tell them the positive things you see. Don't ever be afraid to tell people what they are doing right. *Tell* your husband when he is being a good listener. *Tell* your child when his kindness is coming through. *Tell* your friend when you feel her sensitivity.

If you're serious about helping someone in this area, review the tools of caring discussed in chapter 7. Then, when you are with that person, affirm the tools you see in his or her life. Some of the tools may be rusty or covered with mud, but if you see them in any form, let your friend know. God may use your encouragement to challenge that individual to clean up the tools and use them more often. Your positive attitude will be the most caring thing of all. People are usually well aware of their faults and shortcomings. But most of us are starved for feedback which says we're doing something right.

Sandy often says something like, "It is helpful to me when you put the paper down when we talk." She says this just after I have put the paper down, not when she wants me to put it down. Her gentle reinforcement helps me to be more aware the next time. I can once again discard the offending newspaper for the sake of good conversation.

Look for every opportunity to encourage your friends or family members in positive caring behavior, even if it is not natural for them.

There may be times when you will care for friends who need you very much, but don't believe they have anything to offer you in return. Pride says, "I'll be top dog. I'll keep them dependent upon me. I want them to think they can't live without me." Don't fall into this trap—and don't allow your friends to remain trapped. Let them know what you will be able to receive from them later. They are God's special creation. He has given them some things to offer. Point these things out to them so that they will begin to grow. And guess what? You never know when the roles may be reversed! That is the way it is in God's family. We strengthen each other so that we can serve each other as the need arises.

Challenge People to Try New Things

I never cease to be amazed at my ability to repeat—over and over—things which do not work. This is especially evident in the area of caring. Writing to parents (like me), Paul said, "Fathers, do not exasperate your children; instead, bring them up in the training and instruction of the Lord" (Ephesians 6:4). Doing ineffective things again and again only exasperates! It stands in contradiction to helpful training and instruction.

If you see yourself or your friend engaging in unfruitful attempts to care, it's time to suggest a new approach. After all, practicing a sour note never makes it sound better.

Most goals in life, including caring goals, can be reached in several different ways. When you start out caring for someone, you really don't know what will work. It's all trial and error. You try a certain approach a few times, and then when you don't seem to be getting a response, you try something new. Sometimes people forget that. If you're seeking to help people become more caring, a gentle reminder may be in order. They may be discouraged and fresh out of ideas. Take the time to sit down with them and brainstorm some new possibilities. A new perspective could make all the difference. Don't tell them what to do, but ask them if they feel certain words or actions could be helpful. In other words, leave the evaluation and the final choices to them. When you do this they will feel as though they are learning for themselves, not just following instructions. Encourage them to develop their own ideas and to use these first. They know themselves and the person they wish to care for better than you do.

People who are trying to become caring people may be under stress because of their failures in this area. One of the characteristics of stress is an inability to make decisions. You can care for them by being patient and by helping them come up with new ideas. Encourage them to try out their ideas, offering yourself to hold them accountable for putting some of them into practice. You may also decide to ask the other person to hold *you* accountable to try some new things in an area where you are weak. In doing this, you will care for each other.

Take the Risk of Sharing Your Need to Be Cared for in Certain Ways

One of the most difficult things I have ever done was to tell Sandy that I needed her to hold me in the midst of an emotional crisis. I'd never asked *anyone* to do something like that. I grew up believing that Christians simply don't have that kind of need. How wrong I was. Since that experience I have become much more open in expressing my needs—and she has become much more able to meet my needs. You can help your spouse or friend to become more caring by telling them some specific ways that they can care for you. It will not only be helpful to you but it will also help the other person to see some of the variety of ways in which people need to receive caring. This will increase their repertoire of caring responses and better equip them to reach a hand to others.

Some time ago an acquaintance took the risk of telling me how badly he had needed me to reach out to him during a particular time of crisis with his father. I was astounded because I hadn't recognized the need. I had been too wrapped up in my own agenda. As I listened to him, tears filled my eyes. When he finished speaking, all I could say was, "Ron, if

I had been able to see your need I would have reached out. I'm sorry! Please know that if you have needs in the future I want to reach out to you." Reflecting back on this situation, I now realize that Ron and I became friends at that very moment. He told me his need and that helped me to become more aware. More sensitive. I'll always be grateful for his caring honesty.

Having needs is a part of who we are. We need to come to a place of admitting these needs to ourselves and to others so that we can become more involved in informed caring. This is the fulfillment of John's command.

> A new commandment I give you: Love one another. As I have loved you, so you must love one another. All men will know that you are my disciples if you love one another (John 13:34-35).

Reinforce Caring Behavior

This point may appear to be redundant but if it is I offer no apology. You need to hear over and over again how important it is to help people grow by encouraging the right types of caring behaviors. We have discovered several ways of reinforcement which, although quite simple, are often overlooked.

First, learn to say "Thank you!" These are powerful words. We never outgrow our need to hear them. It is a phrase that never loses its power to change behavior. Saying "thank you" when someone is caring toward us costs so little and yet accomplishes so much. Use it! It will help your friends or family members to become the kind of loving people they desire to be.

Second, point out some positive effects of caring behavior. Sandy helps me in this way. "Earl," she says, "John really lit up when you told him you liked his suit." Or, "You need to hug Darlene more often. She needs your touch of approval." This kind of input helps me to become much more aware of my friends' needs. And as I become more aware, I become more caring. Help your friends and family members by taking note of their effectiveness and pointing out how God is using them to care for others.

Third, ask the person whom you are assisting to identify

the positive feelings which he gets from caring. Anytime you are trying to learn a new skill you will be tense and fearful. This tension can rob you of the opportunity to feel good about yourself for the progress you are making. Sometimes having someone ask you about your positive feelings is all it takes for you to heighten your awareness of the feelings. People spend so much time focusing upon negative fearful thoughts. We all need to be retrained to get back in touch with some of the positive feelings.

One day my handball partner said, "You really like Sandy, don't you?" This came at a time when Sandy and I had been going through some conflict. I hadn't even been aware that I was still able to express some positive feelings, but when my friend made his comment, it put a smile on my face. The smile stayed with me the rest of the day. When I got home that evening I was still very much in a positive, caring attitude. That single comment had helped me in my quest to regain a caring spirit!

When James talks about the power of the tongue to bring about evil, there is a strong warning to control what we say. (See James 3:1-12.) I am afraid that in attending to the warning against evil we have forgotten to emphasize the other side of the coin. The tongue, when properly used, is a powerful force *for good*. The passage says that with our tongues we can praise God and we produce refreshment—like fresh water—in the lives of those around us. Why not refresh someone by asking him to identify the good feelings he gets from caring for others? It is so simple and yet so important.

A fourth way to reinforce caring behavior in your friends or family members is to ask them to identify progress in their efforts. It's just too easy for their vision to be filled with the occasional failures. But each time a person really considers the progress he or she is making, that progress is underscored. The likelihood of its continuing is increased.

Just as saying "I love you" to your spouse tends to strengthen your feelings of love, saying "I have progressed in caring" tends to strengthen your desire to care. People are often reluctant to acknowledge improvement for fear of boasting—or backsliding. Let them know that they *need* to acknowledge their progress. And they need to keep watching for more and more of it. Encourage them not to worry about pride but instead to focus on God's promise. Paul said it very succinctly.

> Being confident of this, that he who began a good work in you will carry it on to completion until the day of Christ Jesus (Philippians 1:6).

God is marvelously faithful in helping people deal with their pride. We need to help them develop confidence.

A final way to reinforce caring is to encourage your friends or family members to expand their avenues in this crucial area. Ask what other opportunities they would like to perfect. Challenge them to think of themselves as constantly growing, not as having "failed" or having "arrived." The book of 2 Peter lists several virtues that we are to possess in our Christian lives. Two of these virtues are brotherly kindness and love—both related to caring. We will never have them in full measure . . . but we can grow.

Don't Kill the Grass

Nurturing caring behavior is very much like starting a new lawn. It takes patience and diligence. You can't take anything for granted. My experience as a home owner and my limited experience as a gardener has taught me to watch carefully three vital areas: watering, fertilizing, and protecting the new growth. Each of these areas has its equivalent in human growth.

Let's look first at watering. Water makes growth possible because it transports life-giving materials to where they are most needed. Caring is like that water. You care for others to in turn produce caring behavior in their lives. Your awareness and careful attention to the needs of others will enable them to grow. This includes encouraging, helping directly, and reinforcing the other person. In addition, we need to bathe the other person in prayer.

One caution is in order: It is possible to overwater plants. You can smother them—sap them of their vitality. Some people work so hard to help a friend or family member that they do not allow him to grow. By "over-watering," they kill caring behavior instead of supporting it. Over-watering takes several forms. Some of the most common I have observed are: nagging, over-protection from failure, and not allowing the person to experience his own needs. In other words, it is possible to do so much for people that they actually become weak and unable to grow on their own.

Give water . . . but also give distance.

My friend, Dr. DeLoss Friesen, has often said, "If you are investing more than fifty percent of the effort in helping a person to grow or change, you are working too hard and will probably fail." Plants that have been over-watered become weak and sickly.

A second necessity for growth is fertilizer. Fertilizer provides needed elements which are not present in the soil. The equivalent of fertilizer in human growth may be the modeling or teaching component. People who don't know how to grow may be stimulated by observing the specific behaviors of those who do. A problem arises, however, when you provide more instruction than the person is able to assimilate. I once fertilized my lawn too heavily and left town for the weekend. By the time I returned, the grass was badly burned. In a similar way, if teaching is not assimilated, it can have adverse effects. People may be burned by guilt because of what they have not done. They may be burned with feelings of inferiority or failure. While a little fertilizer produces growth and confidence, a lot of fertilizer may produce discouragement.

Do fertilize . . . but do it a little at a time. Watch for signs of "scorched" or overwhelmed plants. The more you fertilize the more you may need to water. Caring helps make instruction more absorbable. Instruction without caring may result in damaged plants. The keys are balance and moderation. Observe your garden carefully so that you can provide what is needed. If you make a mistake, don't be afraid to talk to the person about it. If you give too much instruction, be sure to remind the person to take one thing at a time. If you feel that you have smothered someone with caring, talk to him or her about it. Tell that person you need his guidance—that you're willing to back off for awhile. It may be very frightening to talk to someone in this frank manner, but you will find it very helpful. To both of you.

A third need in successful gardening is the new growth of the plants. When I walk through a garden I find that I have huge feet. If I am not careful, I will crush some of the tender green seedlings. This happens in human relationships as well. I may trample through criticism or a negative spirit. Looking out for one plant, I may inadvertently drop my number-tens on another. I must constantly be on the alert to avoid hurting feelings or destroying what the person is learning.

The best way I have found to avoid trampling is to give the person time and space. The more time I spend wandering aimlessly through the garden, the greater the danger I face of crushing tender plants. The solution? Once you have planted, watered, and fertilized, *back off*. Watch from a distance until you can tell that more water is needed. Remember, although you are important to your friend, you also need to work yourself out of a job. The final test of helping someone to grow is enabling him to do it on his own.

Helping others to become caring people is one of the most exciting aspects of relationships. By modeling caring behavior and carefully encouraging and reinforcing the person's growth, I am learning to be more caring myself. When you invest in others, you get good returns on your investment.

Epilogue

Caring Can Change
Your Life

In this book I have sought to share some of the adventures God has taken Sandy and me through during twenty-three years of marriage. We've learned many lessons—at times hard lessons—about caring for one another, and it has been our desire to pass those along. God has helped us move through some changes in the course of our years together—and we like those changes. Sometimes that process has been painful. We've been stretched to the limits. However, as we have assessed the situation, we have both agreed that we would not have had it any other way.

God is a faithful God who leads us in the paths of righteousness for His name's sake. One of those paths is the path of caring. We wander from the path often but are always overjoyed when in our darkness we stumble back onto His way. His mercy endures forever.

Try the path. No, it is not always clearly marked. There will be times when you will feel lost and frightened. During these times, however, you may reach out for the strong hand of your Guide—the very One who created the path. He will not leave you stranded. Those who seek to care will never lack His care. Not for a lifetime. Not for eternity.